Albert E. Scheflen, M.D.
with
Norman Ashcraft, Ph.D.

HUMAN
TERRITORIES
how we behave
in space-time

A SPECTRUM BOOK

PRENTICE-HALL, INC., ENGLEWOOD CLIFFS, N.J.

Library of Congress Cataloging in Publication Data

Scheflen, Albert E
  Human territories.

  (A Spectrum book)
  Bibliography: p.
  Includes index.
  1. Personal space. 2. Crowding stress.
I. Ashcraft, Norman, joint author. II. Title.
HM291.S29   301.1   75-20472
ISBN 0-13-447656-5
ISBN 0-13-447649-2 pbk.

© 1976 by Prentice-Hall, Inc., Englewood Cliffs, New Jersey

A Spectrum Book

10 9 8 7 6 5 4 3 2

Printed in the United States of America

Prentice-Hall International, Inc., *London*
Prentice-Hall of Australia Pty. Ltd., *Sydney*
Prentice-Hall of Canada, Ltd., *Toronto*
Prentice-Hall of India Private Limited, *New Delhi*
Prentice-Hall of Japan, Inc., *Tokyo*
Prentice-Hall of Southeast Asia (Pte.) Ltd., *Singapore*

DEDICATION

TO ALBERT EINSTEIN

Einstein was the most important spokesman in the greatest conceptual revolution since the age of Socrates, Plato, and Aristotle. His ideas altered our views of the world and revolutionized the physical sciences. But we have hardly begun to apply this insight to the study of human behavior. We must, however, unless we are to wallow in our own myths.

contents

preface

The Emergence of a Territorial View

In 1903 a British ornithologist, Howard, noted that birds defined and used small spaces that he called "territories." By the 1960s many biologists had described territories for many species of animals,* and in the decade that followed some authors began to write about human territories.

The rapid spread of interest in territories accompanied a slow-moving revolution in science. This revolution can be traced back to Liebnitz and Maxwell, but it was Einstein who gave it form and direction. And since Einstein, field approaches have developed in many sciences. One can assume that Howard's discovery of territories was one reflection of this critical period in the history of science.

Since the turn of the century field constructs have taken hold and emerged in newer forms, such as cybernetics and general systems theory. These approaches fostered an interest in space-time frameworks and thus in territoriality. And the emerging interest in territoriality may have influenced and facilitated the development of sciences that are based on space-time observations. In any

* Howard (1903); Wynne-Edwards (1962); McBride (1964); Lorenz (1966).

event, the science of territoriality grew within the new thought and the story of territoriality is as well the story of a new way of thinking about our universe.

It is surprising, then, that space-time constructs were last applied to the study of man himself. In fact, even now the science of human territoriality is most rudimentary. Man does not seem to like radical and uncustomary views of his own behavior.

My own involvement in territories began in the 1960s when the anthropologist Ray Birdwhistell and I worked together in studying small-group communication. Ray used to point out the territorial aspects of the behavior we were observing. Often the anthropologist Edward Hall was a welcome visitor, and we would talk about interpersonal space and how it could be studied. We knew that the behavior of spacing and the behavior of communication were somehow interrelated.

In 1966 I went to California for a Fellowship at the Center for Advanced Studies in the Behavioral Sciences. That year two ethologists, Glen McBride and I. Charles Kaufman, were also at the Center. We talked for months about animal territories and looked at films of animals moving and spacing themselves. That same year violent racial confrontations broke in San Francisco. The psychiatrist Jolie West and I became interested in what had happened. Among animals, disruptions of territoriality lead to violence. So perhaps territorial disruption was also involved in crime, murder, riots, and other problems. Certainly, the territoriality of cities like San Francisco is disrupted.

I went to New York in 1967 because Israel Zwerling of Bronx State Hospital and Albert Einstein College of Medicine and Frances Beatman and Stanford Sherman of Jewish Family Service expressed an interest in the study of urban territoriality. The Metropolitan Studies Section of the NIMH provided a grant to study urban territoriality. So a group of us went to work studying apartments, streets, and neighborhoods as territories.

Our study of territoriality encountered serious theoretical problems for very little is known about human territoriality, especially the territoriality of mobile groups and unfixed spaces. The psychologist Adam Kendon and I took and studied motion pictures and video tapes of assembled groups in public places and private households. By 1973, we were able to articulate something of what we had observed. Later we were joined in this effort by Robert McMillan, then a graduate student in psychology. In 1974 Kendon moved to Australia and the collaborators in this aspect of the research agreed to report their findings separately.

The Collaboration on This Volume

During the last years of the project, the anthropologist Norman Ashcraft joined our team as a part-time researcher, bringing an anthropological perspective to our efforts. Occasionally, he participated in shaping the basic ideas being developed by Kendon and Scheflen. Ashcraft participated in two practical ways. His academic training has not obscured his ability to observe human behavior and he has a good sense for context. When Kendon left the project, Ashcraft joined Scheflen in completing the earlier drafts. Since Ashcraft was not in on the original development of the basic constructs in this book, he has declined co-authorship. The authorship is thus attributed to Scheflen, with the assistance of Norman Ashcraft.

With this book we hope to avoid the ponderous and frequently unreadable textbook. We have borrowed from and attempted to improve on the text with a photograph format used in Scheflen's *Body Language and Social Order*. But, we have sought a higher quality of photographs combined with a more conversational style of writing.

By interweaving pictures with text, we sketch the broad outlines and frames of human behavior. It is rather like an art exhibition in which only frames and their configurations are displayed. We limit details, since with a picture of the forms, a person can fill in the pictures of content he already knows.

acknowledgments

Most of the ideas in this book were worked out with Adam Kendon. Valuable contributions were also received from Victor Gioscia, Ron Goodrich, Robert McMillan, Clarence Robins, Joseph Schaeffer, and Randy Sherman. Kenneth Gospodinoff aided us in many ways, especially in preparing the manuscript. We owe much to Bonnie LeCount who not only typed the manuscript, but also supported our work with patience and good humor.

The concepts and photographs in Chapter 8 were contributed by Eve Neuman. With few exceptions, all other photographs were taken by Stan Dworkin and John A. Sergenian. We have noted in the text the few cases where other photographs were used. Diagrams were contributed by Jeanne Bouza.

There were other people who did not work with us in our lab but who helped make this effort possible. The Metropolitan Studies Section of the National Institutes of Mental Health funded most of the research project through grant numbers RO1 MH15977 and RO1 MH18162. Elliot Liebow, Jane Schulman, Matthew Dumont, Maury Lieberman, and Edward Hall of this Section gave us personal support. The Van Amerigen Foundation also helped fund our project. Lilly Auchincloss and Hod Gray of this foundation took a personal interest in our research. Frances Beatman and Stanford Sherman of Jewish Family Service were always encouraging.

The Albert Einstein College of Medicine administered our research grants and the Bronx Psychiatric Center kept a roof over our heads. But it was Israel Zwerling of these institutions who freed us from administrative details, encouraged our research efforts, and helped see to our needs.

introduction:
what is territory?

In the course of evolution, animals have acquired the ability to bound space and time. The territory is an example of bounded space and the calendar is an example of segmented time. In this book, we will deal mainly with territories. We will describe these in relation to traditional segments of time, but we will not say much about other forms of time. These have been described by others such as Gioscia and Floyd.*

A territory is not usually a physical thing. It is formed and used by people but it is not made up of people. In fact, it lies between, around, and among them. A territory is instead a relation or pattern of human behavior and movement.

If we are to visualize a territory, then, we cannot take the usual thing-centered or person-centered view that we favor in everyday life and in the classical sciences. We must take instead a relational or field-centered view—the kind that emerged with the work of Einstein and has been carried forward in some versions of systems theory and cybernetics.

Here in this introduction we will say rather simplistically what such a point of view is. Then we can define territories and the subject matter of a science of territoriality. Last, we will outline the scope and format of this volume.

---

* Gioscia (1974); Floyd (1974).

In western societies we are prone to focus on the things and people in a human event.

We walk into a dining room and see the furniture. We observe things, such as chairs and a table and dishes.

But we can also observe patterns or relations. The clustered furniture, for example, forms a rectangle oriented to a center.

We go to a party and see Mary and Tom and Dave, or we see patterns. People move to form a cluster and then another cluster.

Yet at times and less consciously we do focus on patterns and relations. For example, the wife comes home and immediately notices that the coffee table is a hair out of line so she immediately adjusts it. And we look at the great dipper as a pattern of seven stars in a configuration that resembles a ladle or soup dipper. Then we teach our children to recognize this pattern much as we were taught to.

Or consider the pattern of automobile headlights on a highway at night.
We do not see automobiles or their passengers at night from a distance. We see streaks of lights that can be captured as a configuration by taking a time-lapse photograph from a hill.

We are apparently more likely to see relations and configurations when things themselves are hard to see and when the phenomenon is far removed from human and personal experience. But some people do notice patterns of relations among people. The photographer who took this picture is such a person.

(Photo courtesy of Roy Loe)

The Field and Systems Sciences

The bulk of scientific research has been monopolized by a thing-centered or person-centered view point. In Newtonian physics, for instance, stars or planets are the focus. The fact that these bodies move together was explained by postulating that each emitted a force. And in classical psychology we study human experience by concentrating on individual people and then watching what they do, think, or feel.

But Leibnitz, Einstein, and others took an event-centered or field view of the phenomena they observed. So did Howard and others who have described territories. These people "saw" a *configuration of* animals and things. They saw spaces defined by the locations and movements of animals.

Suppose that we have an image of a configuration and have thus caught a glimpse of a territory at some moment in time. We have now only a frozen picture of a territorial formation, the kind a builder makes when he concretizes a territorial form with walls and fences. If we are to appreciate the dynamics of territory, we must take an additional step. Movement and change also occur in configuration. A territory is an event and events occur in a field of other events and they all form part of a field of larger events.

Our goal would be to describe these forms. Changes in the position of a planet, for instance, are usually called motions. But changes in the position, orientation, or relations of persons are called behaviors. These behaviors define and are defined by territories. *The study of human territoriality is the study of human behavior.*

Once we have included motion and change in our reckoning, we have taken cognizance of time. We have now moved toward an Einsteinian approach to human phenomena. If we examine human activities through time and observe that future events or effects feed back upon and influence what is happening now, we take a viewpoint that is exemplified in recent years by the science of cybernetics.

Our approach to the study of human behavior is similar. We notice the particular forms of bounded space that people establish, use, and move about in. These we will call a territory.

But a territory does not exist in isolation. We are not to be satisfied with describing one territory then another, until we achieve a classification of territorial types, as we did in Aristotelean science. Instead, we notice that a territory *is formed and used within a larger territorial field.* And this field in turn appears within a still larger field. So we can observe that territorial fields lie within and are shaped by larger fields, just as Einstein determined that astronomical fields occurred in still larger astronomical fields.

A larger territorial field is not simply an environment. It is, in fact, a more extensive and often a more lasting field of relations of movement and other behavior. A larger system of behavior like this is called a "context." And a context—i.e., a field of behavioral relations—occurs within some still larger context. We say, then, that contexts are organized in a hierarchical way; and once we have described territories in this way, we have used the methods of the systems sciences.

What Behavior Is Territorial?

Since we are to deal with behavioral fields, we cannot limit our study to the fixed and built territories of man. These are simply concretions of a territorial field set down in a blueprint at some moment of time and built into a cenotaph that represents some past pattern of relations. We will also have to deal with territories formed by orientations and other body movements.

Now we can hazard a preliminary definition of a territory. It is a unit of space defined for a time by some kind of human behavior. Accordingly, then, a territorial behavior is a behavior that defines a unit of space for a while. And the term "territoriality" refers to the processes by which such behaviors are observed and described. But we soon reach an important question. Which of all human behaviors are "territorial"?

The answer will prove to be relative. Some human behaviors are obvious in the sense of bounding, marking, and defending a unit of space. But any behaviors will maintain or change the human definition of spaces and events. So all behaviors are territorial if we look at them from a territorial point of view.

In other words, *territoriality is a way of looking at human behavior;* it is *not* a type of behavior. Behaviors can be territorial, communicational, social, biological, or whatever, depending on the frame of reference a person employs. Intellectual categories are relative to observational time, point of view, and the astuteness and indoctrination of the observer. Often they represent none other than different traditions of study or academic departments of universities.

The Scope and Format of This Volume

In this book we will deal mainly with small, transient territories, for these have been neglected in past studies of territoriality. And we will stick almost exclusively to the territories formed by humans. We use levels rather than classifications or abstract types to determine the division of sections and chapters. Each chapter will describe a level of behavioral integration. We begin with the smallest and briefest units of behavior in space-time and move chapter by chapter to larger and longer units. Our goal is to build a picture of how small elements are integrated into larger and larger ones. Within each chapter, we describe first the behaviors that we think define spaces. Then we discuss how these are sequenced in time to form a temporal unit. And finally, we close each chapter with a brief description of the quantum of space that is thus defined for an interval of time.

We have a great many observations to report and the reader may have difficulty remembering them as we move from small and simple units of action in space-time to larger and more complicated ones. Later in the text we introduce coding systems to identify and help us remember the many units of space-time that people form and use. It will be several chapters before we introduce this device. The casual reader may even wish to ignore it and so we have given this code a secondary position in the exposition.

PART I

TERRITORIES
OF
ORIENTATION

Sometimes people occupy a space, orient their whole body to a focus, and use all the parts and regions of their bodies in a single form of activity. In such cases their movements and orientations define a small temporary territory consisting of the space they occupy and the space they claim.

But we cannot begin our study of territoriality at this level, since people also define much smaller spaces by the placement and orientation of a single body part. They deploy only a hand, for instance, or they focus only their gaze at a particular point. Or they position their head or torso, and try to command a particular area with this pose.

Hence, before we discuss the level of personal and interpersonal space, we must distinguish two levels of micro-territorial behavior. We will call the smallest of these the "level of point units" and the level of body regions will be called the "level of positional units." We will take four chapters to describe the point behaviors of mini-spaces of body parts, and two others to describe the positions and orientations of body regions. Then in Section II we will describe the territoriality of actions involving the entire body.

9

_____ ONE

points and spots

Small parts of the body may be used to claim a quantum of space. These parts move within a small space and point in some direction. So we will call these behaviors "points." This term conveys the direction of such actions and it also indicates the minuteness of the activities in space-time.

After we illustrate some of these point behaviors, we will discuss how they are sequenced and bounded in time. Then we can describe point *units* of behavior.

Point Actions

ACTS OF REACHING AND TOUCHING

Among their many other functions, the hands are used to reach out and grasp objects. This permits a person to claim temporary possession of an object. When he is alone, he can manipulate objects by a series of customary, and familiar acts.

Tactile acts enable a person to make much more direct claims. Here in the illustration the clothing of another person is being grasped and manipulated. Similarly, the body of another person can be touched, stroked, or held.

Other parts of the body are also used to reach, push, bump or otherwise manipulate objects and other people.

A subtle elbow movement can be used to claim room in a crowd, for example, as in the accompanying photo.

There are other kinds of reaching out.

Tactile behavior can be initiated with shoulder or elbow, or with thigh, knee, or foot.
At right, a lover probes for foot contact with his partner.

In this illustration the head is flexed backward and the lips are protruded and thus asserted and puckered.
The closed eyes could be interpreted as equivalent to saying that the puckerer will not notice the kiss as a territorial violation.

These behaviors invite a suspension of privacy. If they are reciprocated, a mutual territory can be established.

Small parts or slight movements of the body can be oriented, aimed, and displayed.

A gaze can be used to warn, call attention to a misbehavior, bring another person to heel, and otherwise control a situation.
In this case the eyes can make a "piercing" point. By holding and exaggerating such a stare, a person can be sure it will be noticed.

An ear can be pointed by turning and cocking the head. So can the mouth.
The genitals, too, can be aimed and displayed by positioning the pelvis and spreading the thighs. Breasts can be protruded.

Points or displays can be accentuated by using the hands. The finger, for instance, can be pointed at the ear. Such a gesture often is used to command attention or request the right to speak.

Certain spots of the body are displayed by gestures or gesticulations.

In courtship and greetings the palm is displayed.* The palm in these cases *is accurately aimed.*

The displays we call "facial expressions" also can be oriented and aimed. The brow, the eyebrows and eyes, the lower face, the mouth, the jaw, and other parts of the body are used in such displays.

Notice here that a constellation of displays may indicate non-comprehension. The knit brows are the most prominent feature.

Such displays can be accentuated by calling attention to them. The point of display can be jutted forward or pointed to.

_____

* Kendon and Ferber (1972); Eibl-Eibesfelt (1970).

Pointing can be directional in every sense of that word. The head toss, face point, gaze, voice projection, hand, and foot can be pointed to accentuate displays.

The point illustrated here indicates to a visitor where she is supposed to sit. It is amusing to *see* people do this while simultaneously *saying* "Sit where you like."
By a sequence of eye, hand, and head points, a figure of authority can position an entire assembly and cue who is to speak and when they are to begin.

The voice is projected and aimed by aiming the head, speaking loudly or softly, and focusing the gaze.
If the voice is projected beyond a listener, he is likely to lean or step backward. If the voice is projected to a spot short of him, he may step forward.

Spots

The point action originates at a small point on the body surface and is directed at a small focus somewhere else. We use the term "spots" to identify these small two-dimensional spaces that become the territorial extensions of the point action. Being only a few inches in diameter, spots can occupy spaces on body surfaces, some other kind of surface, or even in the air. Just as body parts are used for pointing, so do they become spots. There are spots on the body surface defined only by a rash or cosmetic mark. A person may define such spots by stroking, or scratching them, and others may define them by gazing at them.

The eyes, mouth, palm, and ears are spots. So are the lower sides of the face and the brow. Each is a tiny site of expressive or communicative behavior, and each is thus regarded in communicational activity.

In short, the surface of the body is the site of a number of territorial spots. Some are characteristically spots, but any small region of the body can be treated as a spot. The breasts can be used to point. They also can be a spot at which to gaze or avert eyes, depending on the situation.

There are imaginary spots everywhere. While telling an embarrassing anecdote, a person may stare at an imaginary spot on the floor. The listener is likely to avoid looking at this spot. He may stare at one in the air above the speaker's head.

In coming up with a sage remark or in showing that one is thinking deeply about a problem, people stare at spots on the ceiling.

In cultures in which high degrees of eye avoidance are characteristic, each participant in a conversation stares at a different spot. Then each changes his spot of focus at the same time to avoid meeting each other's gaze.

People also define spots on the surfaces of furniture.

At a bar one takes and is granted private spots for change, cigarettes, drink, and hands.

In the household members have sets of spots too.
The husband has a spot for his pipes, the wife a spot for her notepad. On the cocktail table each guest can claim a spot or two for cups or glasses.

Every person has a number of spots for personal articles or even for himself. This is true of body spots also. We must, then, speak of systems of spots, since, in the course of an action, they are used one after another, and since their use depends on the occasion.

Point Units

Sometimes an orientation is established, a brief point action or display is carried out, and then the orientation is broken. For example, a person can gaze at another person for an instant, smile briefly, and then look down and away. The hand can be raised, the palm flashed, and the hand dropped.

But sometimes the point of orientation is held for a moment and a customary and complex *sequence* of behaviors is performed.

This mother holds her child's coat with her left hand, directs her gaze at the activity, and begins buttoning the coat. She buttons first one button and then another.

Then she brushes the spot she has held with her hand, straightens up, and pats the child's head.

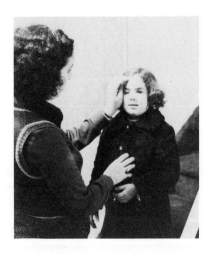

A speaker will orient his head and his gaze *and hold this orientation* until he completes a statement. In this point he may utter a sequence of several sentences and then drop his eyes to discontinue the point.*

The hand is used in a similar fashion. It is held in the air until a sequence of movements is completed. Here is an example.

A man points his gaze and his index finger. Then he thrusts the pointed finger forward.
So far we cannot recognize the sequence, for only its first two acts have been performed. But notice what the man does next.

He turns his palm toward himself so that the back of his hand is directed outward. He closes his fist and points his thumb and jerks it toward the door as he also says, "Get out."

This sequence of points forms a customary and familiar unit.

* Birdwhistell (1966); Scheflen (1972, 1973).

The entire gestalt, including its form and sequencing, direction of the points and the utterance is what makes the point unit recognizable. *Thus recognition depends on a configuration of forms through time in a context.*

But a foreigner might still not recognize this point unit if it were not customary behavior where he came from. And even if he did recognize it, he might be unsure of its meaning.

The cultural setting, too, is a very broad context. In sum, the point occurs *in* a situation *in* a relationship *in* a cultural tradition.

THE MARKERS OF TERMINATION

This point unit and others occur within a space—a space taken over and held for the duration of the performance. We will not notice this as a particular space after the act is completed.

In our example, the man held his fist and thumb in position and space until the other person left. In this instance, the space and the orientation of the point were held until an expected response occurred. Then, the man would turn away and drop the hand.

Thus, the unit of action is bounded in both space and time. *

THE IMMEDIATE CONTEXT

Each of these customary point units occurs within some larger configuration of behavior that is itself a spacially and temporally defined unit. And this unit occurs within some still larger one. In short, "the context" of any element has a spatial-temporal definition. We can use this feature later to order the contexts of an event.

---

* Structuralists have shown that all sequences of action are marked in analogous ways. M. Harris (1964) described this kind of segmentation in time for physical task behavior. It was demonstrated generations ago for speech: the head, face, eyes, and mouth are positioned. A sequence of traditional words are uttered and projected. Near the end of the utterance, the pitch is lowered (in a declarative); a body part is lowered, and the voicing ceases. If the speaker is not to continue, he will then drop his eyes and head and maybe he will fold his arms and sit back (Birdwhistell, 1970; Scheflen, 1972, 1973; Kendon, 1973).

TWO

connections and junctions

A person can perform some conventional point unit without having anyone else share it or respond to it. But sometimes people engage together in point actions. In this case we will say that they form a "connection."

Each of these units of behavior takes a customary form in a particular tradition. These customary units of action have a usual sequencing, duration, magnitude, and shape.

CO-POINTS

Sometimes people take the same point action at the same time. In this case they co-point in a synchronous way.*

Both may turn their heads in the same way *at the same instant.* Then each may gesture and start to speak in exactly simultaneous rhythm.
People often move synchronously while they orient in the same direction.

Often listeners will gesticulate just as the speaker does. Or listeners may beat the cadence of a speaker's utterance by nodding or tapping their feet in a rhythmical way.

---

* For descriptions of synchronous movement, see Condon and Ogston (1966) and Kendon (1970).

In linking, people employ point units mutually and toward one another. A well-known example is the fixed gaze. The link is formed when each party looks into the other's eyes.

Staring also links. In the photo the man stares at a woman's pelvis. She does not stare back but she reciprocates by shifting her pelvic orientation and covering her pelvic area. A territorial claim is acknowledged for an instant even in the act of her rejecting it.

Links also are formed by directing the voice toward a listener. By lowering the voice, a listener can often be made to move closer. By raising it, a listener can often be forced to move back and away.

The hands, too, can be used to form links, or, as seen earlier, the palms are aimed mutually in a courtship and in a greeting exchange.

TIES

Ties are formed by tactile contact. Their occurrence indicates a rather close affiliation in most cultures. (See Chapter 5.)

It is common to see two people walking with their arms around each other.

Hand-holding is common when a pair is involved in some social function, where other people are present.

These ties serve notice to any observers that their users are together.

Some ties constitute maneuvers in a larger relationship, but they do not necessarily service that particular social bond.

The chest poke underscores a point in an argument.

The body contact here is a tactic in karate.

These illustrations also show that ties can be formed in face-to-face relationships as well as in side-by-side ones.

The Spatial Allocations of a Connection

Links can occur across a considerable distance.

Here a gaze is held at a distance of many feet.

And in this greeting the palms are directed at each other and mutually displayed at a distance.

In these cases we will say that an axis is formed.* A small tunnel of space can be marked off in this way. This tunnel is treated as a territory. People keep their gaze out of it and they do not walk through such spaces.

---

* The term "axis" has been used by Goffman (1963) to describe interactional connections at any level of organization.

In the case of ties, the contact is direct.

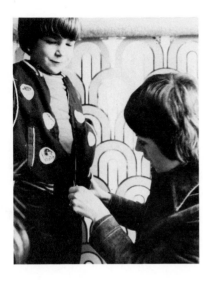

The mother is holding the child's coat as she buttons it. The child is not reciprocating in this case.

Here the grooming is mutual. Each holds on to some item of the other's clothing or body.

In these cases a minute junction of spots occurs and demarcates for an instant a tiny space a few inches in diameter.

Units of Connection

In a co-point sequence, the participants orient in common. Then they perform a series of point units.

Here two people look and listen to a third until he has finished speaking. They hold this orientation together. They nod in unison, smile, exhibit facial displays, and so on.

People can engage in a number of simultaneous link units using their eyes, mouths, ears, and hands to form a pattern of multiple simultaneous link units. Or more than two people can contribute to a set of links.

In an interaction the participants may form one link unit after another.

In courtship, for instance, the gazes are held. Then the participants draw near and form tactile links.

At a next step they link mouths in kissing. But notice that they still hold hands. *So people can employ multiple simultaneous and sequential links.*

It is not feasible to classify these links on only the basis of function. The link does serve in completing a physical task, but the task *and* the link bond the participants together.

The same link can serve metabolic, psychological, social, and economic needs.

In summary, then, the connection is a spatial-temporal unit. A connection is formed by a simultaneous or mutual orientation. This relation of point orientations is held for a while, during which a sequence of point units is jointly performed. Then the connection is broken.*

Furthermore, a given connection will usually occur in a context of other such units. A group of people perform multiple simultaneous and sequential connectional units in the course of an interaction. These configurations of point units and connections will concern us in the next two chapters.

---

* Here we have emphasized the spatial aspects of these connections without detailing the behaviors that comprise them. For more detail see Scheflen (1972, 1973).

———— THREE

positions
and orientational segments

So far we have said that people can use the small parts of their bodies to orient to a focus and thus define small areas of space. Now we must point out that regions of the body can be used in similar ways. For example, the head can be turned without moving the thorax and can be engaged in an activity apart from the activities of the rest of the body. Four body regions of the body can be used differentially in such ways.

This being the case, there is a level at which regions of the body can be used for spatial definition. This level is more inclusive than the level of point behavior that we described in chapters 1 and 2 and less inclusive than the total body relationships that will concern us in future chapters. We will call it the "level of positions."

The Differential Deployment of
Body Regions

Most Americans are highly attuned to the spoken word. Consequently, they are quite conscious of the head and how the face is oriented in human activities. They are less conscious of what the rest of the body is doing. While a person is speaking, the torso, the pelvis, and the legs also are deployed and oriented.

In this case the wife's head and face are turned to address her family while her body is directed to the stove and employed in the task of cooking.

We are forced to be aware that the torso is oriented when we observe a person act as this man is acting.

The mass of his chest and abdomen draws our attention. Its direction is emphasized because of the situation he is addressing and because he retroflexes his spine and thrusts out his torso.

Thus the head-neck region and the trunk can be oriented in different directions and committed to different activities. By the same token, *the pelvis and the torso can be separately directed and committed.*

This person has paused to greet a friend. His upper body is oriented to the friend, but his lower body is still pointed in the direction toward which he was headed.

The orientation of the pelvis is more obvious when a person is sitting down. The pelvis is set forward and the thighs are directed upward. In this way an angle of thigh and pelvic placement frames a sort of trajectory of pelvic orientation.

Here is an obvious example. The man in the center directs his head and torso to the man on his left, but his pelvic-thigh placement is directed to people across from him. An imaginary extension of the angle of his thighs "includes" those persons across from him.

People can even direct their pelvic-thigh region in one direction while they orient their lower legs and feet in another.

In standing, the feet can be oriented much like the thighs. They are splayed to form an angle which can then be directed.
Usually the lower-leg and foot region is oriented in the same direction as the pelvis, but it does not *have to* be, as in the case shown here.

When people are seated with their legs and ankles uncrossed, they can also splay their feet to form an angle. And this angle, too, can be oriented to a place or to another person, as this person is doing.

We have tried to make two points simultaneously. We have claimed that four regions of the body can be oriented and that each of them can be oriented separately. It is thus possible for a person to make as many as four simultaneous but different orientations. But two are more usual.

Within any of these regional deployments, a configuration of point units can be performed.

While the head is held in a certain position and oriented to a particular listener, the eyes can be focused *and* the voice can be projected *and* the brow can be used for display, and so forth.

And while the thorax is held in a given position, the hands can be used for gesticulating and then for lighting cigarettes and then for gesticulating and so on.

In fact, the deployments can be quite complex. The head can be committed to one relationship while the thorax is committed to another. And even within a single positioning of the head, the eyes can be used in one activity while the voice is used in another.

The Spaces Occupied by Body Regions

Each region of the body must of necessity occupy a rather fixed quantum of space.

CUBIT SPACES

The width of the torso and pelvis are each about 18 inches in a full-grown adult human. The widths of the two lower legs and of the head are narrower, but the head is tilted in a wider arc and the feet are often spaced apart. These regions, too, occupy a lateral space of about 18 inches in stationary activities.

The finger tip to elbow distance of the average adult is about 18 inches. So is the distance from heel to knee and from knee to pelvis. The torso is somewhat longer and the head-neck region is shorter.

The average adult body is close to 12 inches thick. When the forearms are extended, the torso occupies a space of about 18 inches.

This space also describes the interior width and seat height of traditional British-American chairs as well as other built lo-cations (see Part III). A measure approximating 18 inches has been important in architecture since ancient times. It is called "the cubit." Ancient Egyptian cubits were over 20 inches in length. The old English cubit is 18 inches.

In the diagrams here notice how cubit spaces describe the relations we have been discussing. In stationary activities, each body region occupies about a cubic cubit of space, but these 4 cubics are distributed differently according to a person's posture.

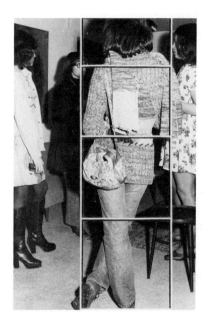

A person stands in a square cubit and is 4 cubits high.

A person sits in a chair a cubit in space, but normally he also has a forward cubit for legs and feet or for leaning forward and a cubit of space to the rear for leaning backward.

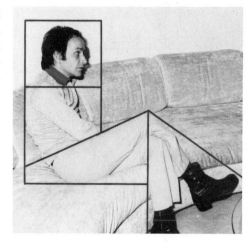

The entire body, then, can be contained in a quantum of space about 4 cubits in size. Ordinarily a person occupies more space than this, as we will describe in Chapter 7.

Stance and Orientational Segment

We have said so far that each body region or cluster of body regions can be oriented. It will be aimed somewhere or toward something or someone. *The position thus commands a segment of space beyond that occupied by the body region.*

At any instant, this segment of space will have a scope—i.e., it will be broad or narrow. The scope is delimited and indicated by the way in which the body region is held.

For example, a person can take in a broad orientation with his head by holding it back and by sweeping it and/or his eyes back and forth.

Or, a person can restrict his orientation by bringing his head forward, holding it and his eyes steady, and using his hands to frame his face and mark off a limited vista.

We will use the term "stance" to describe the way in which a body region is deployed and framed by the hands in marking off an orientation segment.

The thoracic orientation can also define a narrow or broad scope. The two photographs below depict contrasting extremes.

In similar ways the focus of the pelvis and upper legs and the focus of the lower legs can be narrow and exclusive or broad and inclusive. Males widen a lower body focus by slouching in their chairs and spreading their legs.

Each region of the body can be oriented in such a way that it invites, facilitates, or holds an interpersonal relation. Or, it can be oriented in order to break off, discourage, or avoid an involvement.

In the illustration here a man is scanning an assemblage of strangers. His face and gaze sweep over each face before him. He may thus elicit a return gaze, which can be escalated into an interaction by smiles, words, winks, or courtship displays.

But this head is averted. The face is covered. The possibility for an interaction is denied.
Of course, more aggressive intrusions are possible. And a range of intermediate orientations can also occur. For instance, a person can lower his face down and cover it with his hands, but peek out from behind them to glance at other people.

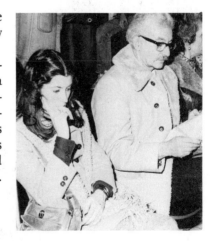

The other body regions can be used similarly to hold or break a relationship.

We use the term "segment" to describe the space that the orientation of a body region covers and claims. Sometimes segments are poorly defined spaces through which people walk and look into without constraint. But when the stance focuses and fixes an orientation, people may avoid walking through it or gazing into it. It is then a territory.

The Positional Unit

In summary, then, a position and stance involve one or more regions of the body and occupy and claim a segment of space for a time.

THE ORIENTATIONAL HOLD

In some activities, the parties keep moving around while they are talking, working, or playing. In these instances a given orientation is not held. But in most stationary tasks and interactions the orientation is "locked in" and held until a particular sequence of behavior is completed.

THE CONSTITUENT POINT UNITS

In performing a physical task, one usually stands or sits with the torso or at least the lower body facing the work area. The head or the upper body may be pivoted to a particular spot while one set of operations is carried out with the hands.

Then the upper body may be shifted to another spot on the work area and held there while some next sequence of steps is conducted.

One acts in a similar way when taking part in a conversation or a meeting.

The body is stationed somewhere and rested on the legs or on a tripod of legs and buttocks. The torso is oriented to the others involved in the situation.

Then the head and neck are directed toward a speaker and held there until he finishes or until he pauses. Then the eyes may be lowered for a second. Maybe a cigarette is lit.

Then the head is swiveled to a next speaker and held there, recognizing that speaker's right to the floor.

Holding an orientation marks the duration of a positional unit, and the orientational segments mark the space used in its performance. By the same token, the shifts in position mark beginnings and endings. So the positional unit is structured like the point unit.

Thus, each point unit is performed in a particular slot *within* the duration and within the orientational segment of the position that is being held. *By the same token, positions are performed in sequence and each of them holds a slot in some larger unit of participation.*

A listener takes one position after another as various speakers hold forth.

Then he sits forward and takes the floor himself. He makes a sequence of points in accord with some logic and then sits back. Still later, he will attend the coffee-break, leave the group, and so on.

FOUR

shared and mutual relations

Two or more people can orient parts or regions of their bodies in such a way that they share an orientation space. Thus they define a space that they use for a joint or a mutual involvement.

Two cases of shared orientational space must be distinguished, for they assume different forms and have a different social significance.

In the first type, the participants merely orient in the same focus of orientation. As they share this focus, they may co-act or behave in unison.

In the second case, the participants come together to form links and orient their body regions *to one another*. Each of the participants holds focus on the other. They are involved.

Shared Orientations

ORIENTATIONS WHICH ARE MERELY ADJACENT

Two or more people may be present in the same place and certain of their body regions may be oriented in the same general direction, but they may not share the *same* focus.

Here, two strangers hold side-by-side seats and thus also share a set of common positions and common directions or orientation. They not only maintain separate visual focuses, but also display this fact with their stance. They place their extremities in such a way as to mark off their foci.

And here, two people are facing each other but they avoid an interaction.

When people merely occupy locations near one another and their positions foster a common orientation, they employ different and separate point behaviors and indicate a separate orientation space by their stances.

Two or more people may move regions of their bodies in unison and share a unified or common orientation. In our research project we code this relation with the letter "u." (We use the lower-case letter to indicate that only body regions share in the orientation).

Consider degrees of this phenomenon. In the least-defined instance, people may not even orient themselves in the same direction.

Here two people are back-to-back watching very different portions of a scene that is going on around them, and we would have no way of knowing that they were sharing an orientation on the basis of a photograph taken at any one instance in time.

But as we watch them through time, we notice *that they track together*. They rotate their heads or torsos at the same time. Ultimately, they turn their faces to look at each other.

At the other extreme, the co-position and unified field of orientation is precisely defined. The regions of the body are parallel in direction and the stance identifies a distinct focus.

Here, two heads are turned to exactly the same spot.

And here, the eye focus and stance define a common and exact focus.

This relation is clearer when the participants turn their body regions in the same direction *and track what is happening in the same time frame.*

Relations like these are formed not only by orientations of the head but also by other body regions as well.

In the case shown here, the torsos are oriented in common.

And in the instance shown here, the pelvises and lower legs are oriented in common.

From now on we will say that the space defined by a confluence of orientations is an "o" space.

A shared orientation does not have to involve the same regions of the body.

In the case shown here, the head of one person and the torso of another are oriented in common to the same scene.

In the simple cases we have described so far, only two people are sharing an orientation, but a great many people can take similar positions and thus share an "o" space.

Here, a row of torsos and heads watch the same event.

The point performances within a shared focus or orientation segment are often "co-active"—i.e., they are of the same general type and they occur simultaneously.

Here, two listeners share common positions, with some of their body parts oriented in the same way. They nod and say "uh huh" together.

When participants co-act, they often take the same stance.
Here, two people watching the same focus assume the same postures with their upper bodies and even hold the same facial set.

Relations involving the same postural stance have been called "parallel" or "congruent" postures.*

_____
* Scheflen (1964); Charny (1966).

In more complicated cases of co-action, the body regions are not used to carry out the same acts at the same time. But the collected actions form a *single part* in a task or an interaction. Said otherwise, two or more people use body regions to do *jointly* what one of them *could* do alone.

Here is a common example. The man prepares to light his cigarette. The woman hastily retrieves one of her own to get in on the lighting. The man then lights her cigarette.
The lighting up process is co-active.

Participants jointly narrate. One supplies the vocal narrative while the face of the other provides a continuing affective commentary.

So far we have described the following phenomena: We have said that multiple people can position their body parts in the same direction and/or the same focus. Those persons who orient in common can take in a broad vista or they can focus to a point or spot and circumscribe this focus by modifying their stance. Partners in an orientation may also co-act.

Bear in mind, however, that we are so far dealing only with common relations of some positions of the body. These same people may simultaneously hold other orientations. This matter will concern us in Chapter 6.

In any event, the shared orientations will claim some degree of space. It may be broad, which is not likely to be respected as a territory; or it may be a focused segment, which is likely to be respected. In the second case, the space is more finite and better defined. In fact, if we take the time to do so, we can measure it.

When people do hold a common or unified "o" space, it has a duration. So this space, too, is a space-time unit within which certain activities will occur. We will say that such a relation and space begins when the first member takes that orientation and that it ends when the last partner abandons that position and orientation. As observers, we may have some difficulty defining and measuring this type of territory, but the participants do not. They readily ascertain the existence of such space even though they may not be aware of it. We can, for instance, see them avoid invading such spaces with gazes and other movements.

Mutual Orientations

FORMS OF MUTUAL ORIENTATION

When people position their body parts at an angle of less than 90 degrees and face one another, they are mutually oriented. This orientation may be "open" at angles of about 90 degrees.

These heads in this illustration are oriented partly toward one another and partly toward other people at a distance. Both parties can interact with each other and with other events as well.

Or the mutual orientation can be "closed"—i.e., it is held at any angle approaching zero degrees.*

These two people are in full face-to-face orientation.

---

* We call this a closed mutual orientation, for full face-to-face orientation occurs in courtship and instances of high mutual involvement. Its occurrence signals a private territory.

The hands can be used to accentuate and display the focus of mutual orientation.

Here, both parties draw near, point their faces and torsos toward each other, and place their hands in such a way as to define a channel of space between them.*

Other body regions can be brought into mutual relation too, just as heads and faces can. Here, the lower bodies of two people are positioned in a stance to form a channel.

In the case of mutual orientations, too, non-analogous regions of the body can be involved. And the relation of mutual orientations can involve many people.

---

* Birdwhistell (1970).

We generalize that an involvement is indicated when two or more people orient their body regions to each other. But *we will not be able to make inferences about the involvement on this basis alone.*

We cannot say that the involvement is sexual or conversational or whatever until we have identified connections and point units that specify such an involvement.
In the case shown here, the links do identify the involvement as a courtship.

And we can only say that *these* body regions are involved for *that period* of time in which this relation is maintained.
Notice that the torsos of these two people are partially involved, but their faces are involved with other parties elsewhere.

We cannot, then, say that people are involved with one another simply on the basis of a transient involvement of certain of their body regions. We can make an assumption of interpersonal involvement only when we have observed these people in larger contexts.

Units of Shared Orientation

SPACES DEFINED BY SHARING

Although shared orientational space may be almost infinite and its boundaries vague, the space in which mutual involvement occurs is finite and definite. It is bounded by the bodies of the participants rather than by an indefinite horizon.

From the standpoint of focus and orientational space, the mutual orientation is more complex and integrated than is the co-orientation, for it consists of multiple directions of orientation *

Bear in mind that these relations include only regions of the body and orientational segments among the people who participate in them. Thus, while one set of body regions forms a temporary area of orientational space, other regions of the bodies of the same people can form other ones. Thus the orientational space among a group of people may have multiple, simultaneous positional divisions.

The concept of degree of involvement derives from Goffman.* (1963).

---

* To distinguish these two levels of relation, we use code terms. We speak of the relation of unified orientations as a "u" relation and the relation of mutual involvement as a "v" relation. We can also use the same term for the spaces defined by these orientations.

* Goffman (1963).

FIVE

with and non-with spaces

In Chapter 4 we described how two or more people could orient parts or regions of their bodies in common. We also discussed two relatively different instances of this configuration. In the first, persons orient to a common focus and co-act toward this focus. We would say that all who share this orientation and co-action are involved *with the same focus*. In the second case, persons orient to one another. They tend to interact, and we can say that they are involved with one another.

But these two ways of organizing interpersonal space do not exhaust the possibilities. Man has two other ways of defining orientational space. The first of these we will call affiliation, or "withness." In this instance, two or more people use parts or regions of their bodies to define *the same orientational* space and thus show that they are together.

In the last of these uses, the participants use their body parts and regions to define *separate* orientational spaces and thus show that they are not together. We will say that these orientations indicate "non-withness," or disaffiliation.

Persons positioned closely together can accentuate their to-getherness by showing that they are sharing exactly the same focus.

Here, two people place their hands to the sides of their faces and thus sharply define a focus of common orientation. By the same action, they show what is being excluded from their orientation.

Furthermore, this use of stance to define a special focus may separate those who do so from others near by who do not specify that particular focus. In this case, two or more people may stand out as being exactly together in some particular point of interest, while the others are not.

Here, two people in the middle of a row of people define a common subfocus within the scope of the orientation of the entire group.

(Photograph by Edward Paul)

People can do the same thing by orienting their torsos . . .

. . . and their lower bodies.

When people assume the same stance with a region or regions of their bodies, we say that they position and orient "in parallel" or that they use congruent body positions and stances.*

---

* Scheflen (1964); Charny (1966).

Stance relations can also be mirror-imaged—i.e., persons can position their outer arms or legs in the same way.

In this case, each person puts his hand to the side of his face. This mutual gesture distinguishes them as a pair, since the raised hands seem to mark an inside and outside.

The legs and feet, too, can be crossed in mirror-imaged stances.

These two persons cross their legs in such a way that their toes almost touch.

When people assume a mirror-imaged stance and turn slightly toward one another, they define spaces among themselves.

In the case shown here, the individuals define such a space with their upper bodies. The outer arms form a ring. A space is partially bounded by the angle of torsos and the line of arm placement even though the heads are not in this instant in mutual involvement.

Here, persons define an analogous space by turning their lower bodies and positioning each uppermost leg.

Notice that these pairs also are closer than the density of the situation customarily requires.

(Photograph by Ed Paul)

More than two people can so define a space.

Here, the two persons at either end assume the mirror-imaged stance and thus act as "book ends" for the whole row.
Huddling and use of the outermost extremities as barriers to others mark off a subgroup.

The legs propped up present a barrier to anyone who might try to enter this row.

People who act this way show that they are "with" one another and thereby not with certain others who are present.

We can also say that the space they mark off in this way is a "with" space.

But notice something important about these configurations. Although the members of these "withs" are using *some body regions of their bodies* to define withness, *they use others to form and hold an involvement with people or events across the way.*

These two listeners form a "with" space as they listen to a third person speak. Their torsos are committed to withness, but their heads are committed to another involvement.

In this picture the pair at the right are still part of the threesome but are momentarily engaged only with each other. Kendon (1972) calls these temporary links "side involvements."

Furthermore, members of a "with" may establish tactile ties while maintaining a mutual involvement with still other parties.

Withness is more than a simple configuration of unified orientation and co-action. Certain other behavior is added to form a "with." In escalating configurations of withness, persons perform the following body stances:

1. They lean or move closer to one another.

2. They use their extremities to mark off spatial boundaries and specific foci of orientation that they share.

3. They turn slightly toward one another (even while involved mutually with other people or events).

4. They form links among themselves through tactile ties and side involvements.

These configurations form, hold, and show involvement *and* affiliation. They are, then, behavioral integrations at a more complex level than either a co-action or an involvement alone. Thus the case of unified orientations, the case of involvement, and the case of withness or affiliation are not merely different *kinds of* relations in a classification of types. *They are successively more organized levels.* Similarly, co-orientation, involvement, and affiliation spaces are successively more organized and complex orientational spaces.

There is' an interesting and inverse relation between the degree of mutual involvement and the degree of affiliation.

At one extreme, a row of people can be highly involved with a person or persons across from them and yet be virtually unaffiliated with one another.

On the other hand, a row of people can maintain a very low degree of involvement with those across from them. Instead, they have an obvious side involvement and thus form an affiliation that is virtually exclusive.

A dynamic relation exists among these commitments. The less the members of a "with" pair are involved with each other, the more they can be involved with third and other parties. These dynamics will concern us in Section IV.

Relations of Disaffiliation

The stance relations that we have described so far indicate some measure of affiliation. They also can be used in opposite ways.

People who occupy the same place may orient in common to a sudden noise or disturbance or to an announcement that concerns them all (as illustrated here), but otherwise they may not necessarily maintain a common orientation or relation.

Even when unrelated people do take a common orientation, they are likely to take a different stance. In fact, they may use their extremities to define separate segments of orientation, as these people are doing.

Strangers or people who have quarreled may use their extremities to form barriers between themselves. So may friends if they are engaged in separate activities.

Here, a conversing pair uses their hands and faces to exclude a third party.

Here, the arms and legs are used in mirror-imaged positions as if to provide barriers between two men who are side by side.

We can notice through time that people who are strangers or those who are acting as strangers studiously avoid holding common and mutual orientations.

SIX

relationships and orientational fields

We have described orientational relations and spaces at two levels of organizations. Those which are defined by small body spots have been called connections, and those defined by body regions have been termed "units of relation."

Each of these descriptions was treated as if the behavior of portions of the body was disembodied. Obviously, total bodies are interrelated in human transactions. We shall use the term *relationships* to describe integrations of the entire body.

Forms of Relationship

MULTIPLE, SIMULTANEOUS RELATIONS

By using their body regions differently, two or more people can hold several different relations at the same time.

CONFIGURATIONS OF RELATIONSHIP

Here, two people hold their torsos and lower bodies in a common orientation to a speaker while they turn their heads for a brief side involvement.

These two people are exhibiting three simultaneous positional relations. Their heads are oriented to each other. Their torsos are slightly turned to each other and they are making tactile holds with their hands. Their lower bodies are averted.

On the other hand, people may commit all their body regions to a common focus.

Here is an example.

Or, like the couple here, they may commit their whole bodies to each other, even though they are among others.

We can summarize some elements in a low-commitment configuration. These are:

1. committing one body region;
2. maintaining a maximum distance from the focus of activity;
3. orienting body regions at an angle such that they are only partly pointed toward the focus;
4. crossing arms and legs or otherwise covering regions of the body;
5. keeping body regions inactive or immobile and thus performing a minimum of behavioral manifestations.

In other words, a minimum number of links and channels are formed in low-commitment states. And the behavioral manifestations are minimal. When speech or gestures are contributed, the voicing may be low, flat, and affectless, and the movements may be desultory.

A low commitment may dissolve the relationships altogether. The group disbands. Or each party turns to a separate focus of attention and neither a co-orientation nor a mutual one is held. We will later call this situation "disassociation."

High degrees of commitment are characterized by:

1. the commitment of a number of body regions;
2. the maintenance of a minimal interpersonal distance;
3. the orienting of body regions at a minimal angle or orientation;
4. the uncrossing of arms and legs and the use of stances that define a sharp and excluding channel of space:
5. an active use of mutual point units and multiple connections and their enactment in an expressive or heightened style.

We can code the levels of orientational relations and relationships with a mnemonic code that will help us remember them.

A unified relation of body parts and co-action is coded "u."

An involvement of body parts is coded "v."

An affiliation of body positions is coded "w."

A disaffiliation of body positions and stances is coded "x."

Relationships among all orientations are coded with the capital form of the same four letters. Thus, the

U relationship is a commitment of the total bodies of two or more people to a common and shared focus;

V relationship is a total body commitment in mutual orientation;

W relationship is a total body commitment to a relationship of withness or affiliation and,

X relationship is a total body commitment to non-shared orientations and disaffiliation.

Naturally, these relations last for a certain period. We can code them in terms of duration only at a particular interval of observational time. Furthermore, they can be mixed in type and they do not have to be symmetrical. Thus, one person can orient in toto to another who merely reciprocates with a gaze or a facial movement or expression.

Units of Relationship

At any instant in time a relationship will consist of a set of constituent sub-units. These sub-units are position and stance relations.

If several people are interrelated, multiple simultaneous relations may exist among them. Suppose we analyze the picture below in this light.

The people at each end of the row of four are holding their upper bodies in mirror-imaged stances and thus mark off a boundary for themselves. This behavior indicates a "with" of "w" relation. The inner pair define themselves as a "with" within this larger "with" by using the arms-around stance and standing very close.

Three members hold a unison ("u") relation with their upper bodies by orienting in common to the fourth member, who is speaking. These three thus hold a "v" relation in a face-to-face involvement. The people at each end are also in a "v" relation. The inner pair hold their bodies in a unison, co-actional, or "u" relation.

Each relational unit is made up of connections.

For instance, the relational unit depicted here is formed by a mutual orientation of body parts and three links: one between hands; one between speech and listening, and one between gazes.

While a relational unit is held, the configuration of links may shift and change.

So the relational unit depicted above looks like this a moment later.
A tactile tie has formed but the gaze and speech links have been discontinued.

A relational unit, too, will be but one of many such relations among members of a group.

Hence, those who held the changing connections in the photograph above are also holding other relations at the same time.

And these relations, too, will shift and change through time.
So the relational configuration above looks like this a moment later.

We will say, then, that the sum of relations that exists among a group of people constitutes their relationship. In short, a relationship consists of many simultaneous and sequential relations.

If we know what the order of sub-units is for a given kind of customary relation, we know when the relation starts and when it is over. Ordinarily, we must establish this matter.

In some cases it is simple to do so. At the exact same instant, all participants may turn, orient a body region to one another, and begin to form connections. But in other cases the establishment of a co-position or a mutual one is not simultaneous.

Here one person turns, holds his gaze, waits, and signals for attention.

Then the other person turns to acknowledge and share the links.

We will say that the positional unit begins when the first body region assumes the orientation and we will say that it ends when the last orientation of is configurations is shifted and discontinued.*

_____
* Kendon and McMillan (1973).

A relationship is framed in a similar way. Although the participants hold some configuration of orientations, they may change the separate relations simultaneously and sequentially. But at some point they break off all of their relations of orientation, links and ties.

The unit of relationship is thus framed by the bodies of the participants and by their forming and breaking the sequence of relations.

Following is a diagram of this larger unit of relationship in space and time:

Relationship A

Relation 1   *Relation 2*   *Relation 3*

We can name these units of time within which a particular configuration of connections and body relations occurs.

We will say that any set of connections, formed and held for awhile, constitutes a step in the event. And a relation of body regions formed and held for a while constitutes a phase in the activity or event. Later on in Section II we will describe stages during which persons hold a particular position before they move about and take different positions.

We can also differentiate sub-units of space in an ongoing event.

At one niche in the total configuration of simultaneous relations a given unit is held. Another was going on in another niche.

In summary, an event can be subdivided into several elements: shifts in positional units, or "steps" in the event; a sequence of such shifts, or "phases" of the event; and "stages" of the event, which refers to any number of phases in the event that are held in the same formation (see Section II).

But all events occur within a larger schedule of events. This schedule is defined by what happened at a place on a given day. In turn, all the events at all sites occurred within a particular institution. And that institution and all others occur within a society, and so on. *The larger events form the contexts for any event occurring within them.*

In other words, a unit of relationship is defined by (1) its constituents, (2) its total gestalt in space and time, and (3) its slot in a larger system of contexts. On this basis, a relationship is recognized, attributed meaning, and judged.

Space-time units of orientation often occur within a cluster of people. Thus a ring of people is formed for a time, and *within* the space defined by this cluster, multiple units of orientational relation and behavior occur.

But sometimes the orientation spaces are cast beyond the confines of the assembled people and sometimes orientations pervade an assembled group. We will describe the spaces of assembled groups in Section II. NOTICE THAT ORIENTATION SPACES AND ASSEMBLY SPACES ARE RELATED BUT THEY ARE NOT THE SAME.

Now we can speak of an orientational field. It is an interdependent configuration in space and time consisting of all of the simultaneous and sequential orientation relations that occur within all the relationships that make up that human activity or event.

An orientational field is not invented for a particular event nor is it a random pattern of spaces and sequential changes. Instead, the spaces defined by orientations conform to standard patterns used among people *in* that kind of activity *in* those sorts of relationships *in* that particular cultural tradition. Thus the same fields are formed hour after hour and generation after generation in place after place in a particular society. The members of that tradition and society learn these patterns and programs, follow them when the occasion demands, pass them on by example, and pass out of them when they die.

In some measure, an orientational field is thus like an astronomical one. Red giants are "born" into it and die out to become white dwarfs, but the space-time structure remains even though its participants change. The orientational field allows man a much wider range of variation and manipulation than a galactic or solar system, but in each case order is maintained.

PART II

FORMATIONS
AND
SITES

So far we have written as though the orientation and relation spaces are suspended in mid-air among people who have only parts or regions of bodies. But obviously these spaces are formed by people who occupy locations on the floor or ground. In fact, the clustering of people itself marks off a kind of claim or territory that is different in form and size from the spaces marked off by orientations.

To describe the clusters people form, we will use Kendon's term "formations." These formations consist of solo locations, rows, files, circles, squares, and other geometric shapes. They occupy and circumscribe a space that we will call a "site." At, around, and within this space certain kinds of human activities will occur. The orientations of the participants will move within, across, and beyond this site.

We will focus on describing formations and sites in relatively open places—in places not organized by walls or furnishings—in order to see how people form territories by positioning and spacing their bodies. Then in part III we will see how arrangements in spaces with furnishings, walls and other barriers replicate the formations that people use in open space.

SEVEN

solo sites or locations

When a person is alone or when he takes part in a group activity involving very few other persons, he or she will occupy about a square meter or a square yard of ground or floor space at any given moment in time. These sites of solo or individual activity will be called "locations."

Defining a Location

THE K-SPACE

When relatively stationary, the body of a full-grown person uses roughly 4 cubic cubits (i.e., 18 × 18 × 18 inches for each body region). The body of a full-grown human occupies about 4 cubic cubits (i.e., about 18 cubic inches for each body region). Thus this space is about 1.5 × 1.5 × 6.0 English feet, or about 0.5 × 0.5 × 2 English yards. Since this space has no common name and since it is a constant, we have dubbed it a "k-space."

In very dense crowds a person may not be able to claim or use a larger space. He must keep his arms folded in front of his body. He cannot spread his arms or legs and must remain relatively immobile.

Normally, even in relatively dense crowds, a person has elbow room, leg room, and space in which to gesticulate and change posture. Normally, at least a 24-inch cubit space is available.

LOCATION SPACE

Under less crowded conditions a person claims and is usually allowed considerably more space than that which is required for the body itself.

At a gathering in open space there will be lateral space at either side of a person. This space may be the size of a k-space. Notice in the illustration here that there is about a yard of space between persons, but each one shares this space. Each person will also have *at least* a cubit of space before and behind him.

The location is often at least four times the size of a k-space and the person has room to step and lean in any direction without intruding on his neighbor's location.

The same amount of space is available in seats in private places. The arms of the chair or the two end locations of the sofa are examples.

Needless to say, the location too, has a magnitude, a deployment, and a system of orientations at any instance in time.

There are two frames of reference that we can use in studying a location. If we concentrate on a person and on where he goes and how he lives, we see that he always has *a* body space. He even holds one after he dies. While alive, we can say that he carries it with him as a portable territory. In this light such terms as "personal space" or "space bubble" have arisen.*

SPACE IN A PLACE

But we are not going to look at the body space in this frame of reference. We are primarily interested in relations and fields of social space. We will describe the space one person uses in a particular gathering in a particular place. This space belongs in the place. If a person leaves that place, he does not take its location with him. Either it disappears when the person leaves or it is taken over by someone else. He may, of course, come back and re-occupy it at some later time.

Thus, in our usage a location is a "hole" in space, so to speak. It is a quantum of space that a person *can* or *may* use. A location, then, is purely relative to how it is defined.

HOW A LOCATION IS MARKED

One way to mark a location is to occupy it, and thus make it a socially meaningful unit.

At low densities, the participants in a group affair will space themselves to allow one another an area of space large enough to shift position, hold possessions and babies, move the arms about, and so on.

This photograph shows the spacing of a conversational cluster. The space between each participant can in some measure be shared, but an unwritten rule constrains the group members from crossing an invisible line between them. Close affiliation and conditions at the place will make for an exception.

---

* Somer (1969).

Sometimes a location is an empty space because it is habitually or customarily used by a particular person or for a particular role. And a location can be reserved by marking it with a personal possession.

Some Features of a Location

The *boundaries* of a location in open space are defined only by conventions of territorial respect and the movements an occupant makes in his place. We will see later, however, that locations are marked by physical boundaries in built space (see Section III).

An orientation will be imputed to a location when it is occupied by a person or an item of furniture.

In a location there may be multiple simultaneous orientations if its occupant orients his body regions in different ways (see Chapters 4 and 5).

Or it may have a single orientation, as we described in Chapter 6.

In this photograph a location is occupied by both a chair and a person, each with a single and similar orientation.

A location has a deployment at any instant of time.

In Chapter 3 we described how a person can take up different positions in a location, and we pointed out that the body regions are deployed differently in standing, sitting, and lying down. In fact, we diagramed these differences, so the reader may wish to turn back to that diagram. But we mean more than this when we speak of deployment.

A person may step forward in his allotted location and thus draw closer to those across from him. This happens during high involvement.

Or a person may lean toward one side of his location and thus draw closer to a person on that side of him than to the person on his other side. This deployment is used in affiliation.

An allocation of locations is made on such bases as status and role. Thus, particular people will occupy particular locations at given activities.

This arrangement is most evident to us in the case of ritualistic activities and in performances and games. The football formation is a case in point. The formation is one of a set of formations. In it there is a set location for the tight end, for the quarterback, and so on.

But order like this prevails in informal groupings and activities as well.

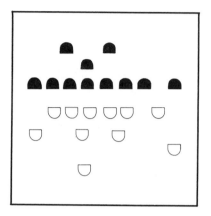

In a ring of people assembled for conversation, for example, a special location is allotted to speakers and to experts or specialists. This location is larger than the others. It is some distance forward from the others, toward the middle of the circle, and so on.

The Location as a Space-Time Unit

The orientations and deployments and actions of a location are of finite duration. They are initiated and terminated at steps and phases of the activity.

The location, too, has a duration. It is taken over and allocated at a stage of the activity. Then it is abandoned.

We can measure the size and duration of a given location if we observe how a person uses it and moves about in it and notice as well how the others stay out of one another's locations.

Such measurements could be recorded in feet, yards, meters, and in clock-time, but we will not deal with such exact figures. We will instead speak *of the magnitude of a location.* We will say that the location one person uses while acting alone in a stationary activity is magnitude 1. A person may sprawl out in a location at magnitude 2. He may move around in larger magnitudes.

Each of the features of a location will vary with the context. They will vary with the immediate degree of commitment.

In situations of close involvement the orientations, actions, and size will have a particular character. In the very close involvement shown here, two people share a single magnitude of location. But in situations of low involvement each person may use a location and one or two location-sized spaces will be kept open between them.

Close affiliates, too, will crowd together in a magnitude 1 location. Strangers will leave at least a cubit or a location-sized space between them if there is room to do so.

Conditions at the place will also determine the characteristics of a location. High noise levels will draw people together. So will heavy crowding.

Still larger contexts also control the allocation of space in a group activity. Cultural tradition is a case in point.

The British, British-Americans, and Black Americans traditionally occupy relatively large spaces. They stand more than 36 inches apart even in fairly intimate conversations if they have room to do so.

But Mediterranean people and Eastern-European people tend to group more closely. Accordingly, each person's location is somewhat smaller.

And Latin Americans tend to huddle together at even closer distances.

Cuban men may stand only 18 inches apart when talking in quiet and uncrowded places. At this distance, the locations of each group member are even smaller.

Within any cultural tradition adaptations are made to activity, density, noise level, and so forth, but these variations are made from and within the cultural norm of that particular tradition.

If, then, we are to describe the form and size of a given location, we must do so in reference to many levels of context.

Thus we can say that a location is about 1 yard square and 2 yards high *if and when* it is (1) occupied by an adult standing male, (2) not with a close affiliate, (3) speaking in conversation, (4) in a quiet uncrowded room, (5) in the British-American or Black American traditions.

A location less than a square yard will probably occur if and when (1) an adult woman, (2) listens in conversation, (3) with a close affiliate at her side, (4) under uncrowded conditions, (5) in these same cultural traditions.

A difference in age group, gender, affiliation, role, activity, setting, class, region, and culture will make a difference in the nature of each location. So measures out of context are meaningless and misleading. Personal space is contextually determined.

EIGHT

dyads

Eve Neuman *

Before we describe types of formations, we shall consider two simpler relationships of people in space.** In one, people who occupy the same area are not involved or affiliated. The other is the dyad, in which two people are mutually involved or affiliated. The study of the simple dyad will prepare us to understand the elements and face formations to be described in Chapters 9 and 10.

Unaffiliated Rows or Sets

Strangers often congregate in the same general area in a public place. They use several means to maximize the distance between themselves and remain uninvolved.

---

* Ms. Neuman, a graduate student at the School of Social Work, Columbia University, had already made such an excellent photographic study of the row and dyad in public that the authors asked her to summarize her work for this chapter.

** These observations were made on a pier in Manhattan. The pier is an open, rectangular walk that juts out onto the Hudson River. It has recently been made a public park. At the pier's end is a wooden bench. Along each side is a raised wooden barrier that also serves as a place for sitting.

They space themselves as far as density allows and place barriers between themselves.

Or they use existing barriers to separate themselves.

Strangers space themselves as far apart as possible *and* orient in different directions if there are no barriers among them.

These two are sitting almost back to back.

People who merely happen to be together in the same place tend to adopt certain characteristic postures.*

---

* Kendon (1973) uses the term "co-presence" when people are uninvolved and unaffiliated in the same area.

They widen their stance so that their knees are pointed outward. They may also put their hands on their hips and thus mark off a broader space with their elbows. They may scan with their faces and eyes but avoid looking into the spaces others occupy. Their backs are often slightly arched.

A second common co-present posture is one in which the knees are retracted and the legs are crossed. The elbows, too, may be retracted. The back is markedly arched and the head may be lowered. The body is curled. In this posture the person is likely to be engaged in solitary pursuits such as eating or reading.

Separate Pairs

The contrasts betwen dyadic and unaffiliated spacing and orientation can be more clearly seen when a "with" or dyadic pair is together in the same space with a stranger or another pair.

Here, a standing pair shares an area of the pier with a solitary stranger.
The pair members cluster together at a considerable distance from the single figure. Each cluster orients in an opposite direction. The male member places his right leg and arm across the space between him and the third party.

In this photo, a pair on our right is grouped closely and partly involved face to face. The third party on our left is oriented away from the pair and uses his left elbow as a barrier against the pair next to him.

In this instance two pairs are in close proximity. But each pair holds a face relation *within* the pair. The pair members nearest the stranger keep their backs to each other.

When pairs and strangers are crowded together on a bench, they will indicate their withness (W) and non-withness (X) relationships.

In this photo, person A is leaning away from B and raising his right shoulder. Person B excludes A with her umbrella. B and C are turned toward each other and C's arm contacts B. C and D are turned away from each other, but D and E exhibit an almost face-to-face withness. F has spaced himself farther from E and is oriented in another direction.

Dyadic or "With" Pairs

Those who are together tend to cluster closely. Furthermore, they tend to co-orient and use parallel or congruent postures (See Chapter 5). Here are three examples:

Sometimes the dyadic members will use mirror-imaged postures and orientations. These may sometimes bring them into face-to-face relation, as shown in the lower photograph.

If there is any doubt about the matter, we can distinguish a "with" pair because the members will leave together. When they do, they will walk in step and move in synchrony.

So far, most of the examples have shown dyadic pairs in side-by-side relationships. In Chapter 9 we will describe this kind of formation as an "element." but, of course, dyadic members can turn toward each other.

Partly, as in this case . . .

. . . or fully, as in this one. We will return to this case in Chapter 10

NINE

elements and modules

If a person occupies a location and orients toward other people or things, that person is but one element in the larger cluster. More accurately, we should say that a person's location, orientation, and activity is but one element in the larger scene.

Often a dyad, row, arc, file, or grid of people stand together and orient in common. In this case the entire cluster may co-act and thus present itself as a single unit of participation. In this case we will say that *the cluster is* an element in the larger formation. We will call the space held by an element "a module."

The Forms of an Element

All members of an element orient in common *and* cluster in an array.

If a number of people orient in common from distant and diverse locations, they co-orient but they do not constitute an element.

(Photograph by Roy Loe)

If people stand in a row or arc but orient to one another, they form what we will call a "face formation" (See Chapter 10).

If they orient in different directions, we will simply say that they are "gathered" (See Chapter 11). In neither of these cases will we use the term "element."

The dyadic pair is a very common variant of the element.

These two women exhibit strong affiliation and they crowd together at minimal distance to each other even though they have plenty of lateral space.

This dyadic element occupies a space no larger than the usual area of a location. In fact, the use of such an increment of space defines them as a highly affiliated pair.

These people hold their affiliation but orient in a common focus to which they co-act. The person who faces them looks at both, includes both in his comments and stance, and otherwise acts as if he is addressing a single social element.

In an uncrowded, quiet place, the members of an element are likely to occupy *adjacent* locations.

Like this . . .

. . . or they may even leave an
open location between them.

But if others who are relative strangers come to occupy the
same side of the cluster, affiliates will draw together to keep their
distance from the strangers. Thus, an element can consist of two
or more pairs of affiliates.

We could diagram a great many variations in the spacing and
deployment of members of a small element.

Variants in Form

The array may not take the form of a small and straight row,
as we have illustrated so far.

One member of an element may
stand forth somewhat to greet,
speak, or form an involvement
while his partner hangs back.
Thus the array is "offset."

Or the array may take the form of a queue or file.

An element may take the form of an arc or a semicircle.

Or the element may take the form of a phalanx of multiple rows and columns. It can be of any size up to a mob or a crowd of thousands milling toward or watching an event.

Here, four young people walk down the street in a row. A fifth walks ahead of the others. The formation reminds us of a parade.

Size is not the critical factor in determining that a cluster is an element. What is critical is that the members have arrayed themselves and *taken a common orientation.*

Relations in an Element

The persons in an element may hold at some phase all the types of relation that we described in chapters 4 and 5.

They may co-act in type "u" relations.

They may turn and be face-to-face in mutual "v" involvement.

They may hold type "w" relations of affiliation *and* type "v" relations of involvement.

Or they may dissociate from each other in type "x" relation.

Modules of Space

We say in our research that an element occupies *a module of space*. A module, then, is the space claimed or held by an element.

In open space the module may be bounded only by relative distances.

Thus the members of one element stand closer to one another than they do to others. Sometimes conventions constrain the rights of people to cross from one element to another (see chapters 10 & 11).

If different elements cluster to form a mutual involvement, each one will have a different segment of orientation and occupy a different side of the configuration.

The space actually occupied by an element may be of almost any magnitude.

If two people crowd into a space the size of a location, the module is of magnitude 1.

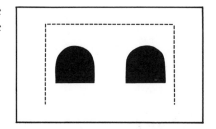

Four people can be crowded into a module this size.

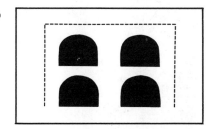

Two people in adjacent locations form a magnitude 2 module.

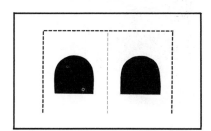

A magnitude 3 module can be used in a variety of deployments.

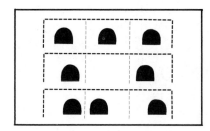

So can a much larger one.

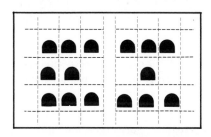

The element has a duration. It is organized at a time, held, and then adjourned. Similarly, the module is claimed, occupied, organized, and then abandoned. *Thus the module is a space-time construct.*

BUT A MODULE IS A LARGER AND MORE COMPLI-CATED AREA OF SPACE THAN THAT PORTION THAT IS OCCUPIED BY PEOPLE.

First of all, it embraces empty locations among the members.

The members also claim a joint "o" space across which they orient and project voices (see page ■).

Around the occupied portions of the module is a small region that is respected by those who pass by. This region is also respected by new arrivals who pause before it as if it were a threshold. It is also used to store the possessions of the members of the element. And the region may also be occupied by a close affiliate such as a spouse.

The region reminds us of the elbow room and leg room of a location. In fact, we will see that all formations have a region.

TEN

face formations and nuclei

People can come together and take up locations facing one another. Or members of an element can turn in their locations and establish a face-to-face relationship. We will use the term, "face formation" to describe clusters such as these.*

These clusters take the shape of small squares, rectangles, triangles, or circles of various magnitudes. A face formation has at least two discernible zones, which we will call the nucleus and the region.

Face-to-Face Forms

The face formation is established when some number of people cluster and face each other. There are several degrees of complexity of these clusters.

In the simplest cases, two people face each other, as we described in Chapter 8.

---

* Kendon (1976).

Three people of roughly equal status and affiliation often form a triangle.

And four can form a small square.

When still more people join the face formation, an expanding circle is formed. This example occupies about 15 square yards.
As the circle grows, the members are spread further and further apart until it becomes difficult to maintain a single-face formation.

When about ten or twelve people have joined the circle to occupy a space of about 30 square yards, the circular form of the face formation tends to become unstable. It may break up altogether. But often it undergoes two forms of change.

The members form separate elements of co-action and/or affiliation around the circle in closely spaced pairs or trios. Or the face formation breaks down into multiple separate clusters *of two or three people* (see Chapter 11). So the face formation of people, like that of animals, has a maximum convenient size.*

----

* Calhoun (1966).

Variations in Form

The size of the space formation is in part a function of the degree of involvement.

In the very high involvement of courtship, the partners may embrace. When they do so, there is no space between them and the entire face formation occupies but a single location.

In close conversation at a lesser degree of involvement, the participants are likely to stand about a location apart.
This, the "o" space, is a location in size and the entire cluster occupies about three locations.

But in quiet places people may stand two or more locations apart. They do so in more formal relationships and in situations of low involvement as well.

The matter of distance is more complicated than a simple issue of involvement.

The face formation will be small even in formal conversation if the noise level is so high that people cannot hear one another, for example. It will also be small if the area is crowded with other clusters of people.

In built spaces, tables and the need for leg room in front of chairs will force the participants to sit farther apart (see Section III). The spacing in a face formation is a complex matter of involvement, activity, and environment.

The study of interpersonal distance is often called "proxemics." * In a systems science distance is examined in multiple contexts.

Other variations in form stem from the posture of the participants. They may not stand, although we have illustrated them standing so far. They may sit on the ground or floor, lie down, or sprawl, but still maintain a face formation.

Variations in the shape and size of a face formation are also occasioned by the fact that there may be open spaces at various parts of the formation.

The Spaces of a Face Formation

We can focus just upon the spaces that are formed by a face formation.

LOCATIONS

In the closest and simplest case, the embrace, the whole formation uses or delineates just a space location. This instance can be diagramed something like this:

---

* Hall (1963, 1966).

MODULES

If the participants are located in rows and there is a vacant location between them, the face formation defines a module of space. These modules can be diagramed at various sizes as follows:

When one side or arc of a face formation is occupied by a closely affiliated pair or set of people, this element occupies a module of space, as we described in Chapter 9. Thus several modules may face one another in the composition of the face formation. This possibility can be diagramed as follows:

THE NUCLEUS

The face formation can thus employ one or many locations or two or three modules around an "o" space.

At some phase in a conversation, the participants in a face formation may pair off and carry on separate conversations. Then the space is subdivided into two adjacent modules as follows:

Or the participants can form channels that cross one another as a square of people talk across one another's orientational space.

Or the participants in a small circle or square can orient mutually and thus establish for a time a unified space that has four sides and a central zone "o" like this:

In any of these cases, if the space is larger than a single module, we will call it a nucleus. The nuclear space of a face formation can be much more complicated than the simple examples diagramed above. It can have more than four elements. It can have elements at each of three, four, or more sides, and so on.

THE ZONES OF A NUCLEUS

Since the participants cluster about a central space of orientation, the nucleus has two subzones, "o" and "p."

The "o" zone. When the participants are oriented mutually, the zone of orientation lies at the center of the cluster. In this case we will say that the "o" space is a *zone*. Into this central zone the participants cast their orientations. Its integrity is protected by rules of convention. *Dogs can wander through it and small children can play there, but no juveniles or adults are supposed to position themselves there or walk through it.*

The members of a face formation will close ranks against anyone who tries to violate it.

The "p" zone. The participants take locations about the "o" zone and thus form elements. Collectively, these modules of space form a strip or zone that holds the main or central participants in the face formation. We call this zone the "zone of participants" or the "p" zone.

THE REGION *

A region is defined under uncrowded conditions by the fact that people who pass by give the nuclear formation berth, usually about a location wide.
Those who pass by also dip their heads and eyes.

* Kendon (1973); McMillan (1973).

Those who approach an established face formation also define an outer region by acting as if there is a threshold behind the nucleus of the formation. They pause a location away and wait to be invited in or make some sign so that some inner member will turn and attend them.

Sites of Activity

From now on we will use the term "site" to describe the total space that is employed in one human get together for one kind of activity.

A site is defined, then, by the fact that the people there are participants. They are affiliated with one another and they get involved with one another or with a common task or transaction.

SPACE DIVISIONS

An element occupies a location or a module of space that includes an orientational space before the element of people and a region around them. A face formation occupies a location, a module, or a nucleus of space. The orientational, or "o," space is at the center since the participants orient mutually. They occupy a zone of central participation (zone "p") and the whole nucleus is surrounded by a region.

In the case of a moving activity, an element uses a path rather than a stationary module. In active play the central participants move around in the nucleus and sometimes in the region, so the zonal divisions are not preserved.

THE TEMPORAL BOUNDARIES

In a stationary face formation, the space is sectioned in various ways as the participants change their orientations from one phase of the activity to the next.

The stages of a site are marked by the appearance and disappearance of a particular kind of formation. We will say that a particular formation begins when its first member takes up a location and orientation in that formation, and it ends when the last person relinquishes the location and orientation he held in that particular formation.

Thus the stages of an activity are held in different types of formations. At stage 1, for instance, a cluster of multiple small face formations may form as people greet and exchange pleasantries. Then a second stage is initiated when one and then another take up positions to form a face formation. And yet a third stage appears if and when the face formation breaks up again into multiple small face formations and elements.

In its simplest form, an activity has three stages: In the first, the people arrive, greet one another, and move about finding locations. The main stage of formal activity begins when a face formation is established and the expected business gets underway. The final stage occurs when the face formation breaks up and the participants part and leave. Sometimes a site is formed only by the first-stage activity, such as a passing encounter or greeting. At other times a succession of multiple stages occurs as one, then another, and still another formation appears and is abandoned. A site of activity like this has *multi*-stages.

ELEVEN

combined formations

We can identify human formations that are more complicated than an element or a face formation. Here we describe three such formations: the gathering, the hub, and the intersected formation.

These formations are combined forms. They are made up of combinations of solo people, elements, and face formations. These combined formations can be quite complicated, even when they are small, and the organization of sites and stages is more difficult to comprehend. But no new principles are involved.

Gatherings

THE SIZE OF GATHERINGS

In a gathering, the participants are together in the same area but they do not share a common orientation nor do they orient to one·another. In other words, they do not cluster in either an element or a face formation but in some combination of both.

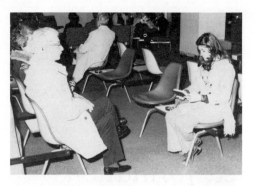

In the simplest instances, two or three people join together in a common purpose, but they do not form an array or share an orientation.

In other instances a face formation breaks down into separate subgroups. The members do not maintain a common square or circle any longer.

Gatherings often consist of less than a dozen people and thus occupy a small common space we will later define as an "area."

Or they can be much larger and occupy a set of areas.

(Photograph by Roy Loe)

Notice multiple subgroups each of which occupies an area.

A gathering may be organized into multiple sub-formations and spaces, each of which has a different status or function.

A powerful or high-status group may form and other small formations may gather around it. This kind of gathering has a nucleus, whereas others have multiple nuclei. Some gatherings contain sub-groups that have special status or play a special *at one end* and thus exhibit a gradient of status. Here is an example.

(Photo by Edward Paul)

Some gatherings reserve areas for conversation, for rough play, for older members, for eating, and so on.

Some gatherings as a whole are mobile, but the sub-groups do not usually move about at random within it.

There is another sense in which a gathering is organized. Since the participants usually have common affiliations, any member can move from one cluster to the other. But in doing so, certain amenities are to be observed. One is not to shout or barge through a sub-cluster, for instance.

Hubs

In a hub formation, the inner and outer zones are differentiated by role and status. People in the nucleus perform to and for those in the region.

SIMPLE HUBS

In the simplest version, only two people are involved. Here, one performs while the other watches.

The person in the center can turn in all directions. In fact, this turning to turn, defines a nucleus in such simple cases as this.

Out of context, there is nothing about these tiny formations which distinguished them from small elements of face formations. We would have to observe their relationship through time and/or study a more complete version of the formation to determine that a hub configuration was evolving.

Several others now join the two people pictured on the page, and an element of spectators is formed.

When a full circle surrounds the central performers, the hub formation is complete.

Notice its characteristics. There is a person or a formation in the nucleus. *These nuclear people orient peripherally and face the region,* or at the least, project their voices to those in the region. Thus *the polarity of the hub is the opposite to that of the face formation.* The focus of the activity in the nucleus is outer-directed or centrifugal, aimed at those in the region.

MULTI-ZONED HUBS

The part-hubs and hubs shown so far are simple. They consist of only two zones of people. There is a nucleus and a region. In more complicated hubs *the region* is subdivided into an inner or outer regional zone and an outer zone of spectators. This subdivision we will call the "surround."

Here the child locates herself in the nucleus and shows off for a ring of guests in the surround. Her teacher takes an intermediate or regional position, monitoring the act.

Notice again a variation we have already mentioned. The nuclear performers can turn outward to the audience or stay in face formation with one another. The nuclear formation may be a single person, an element, a face formation, or a gathering.

A number of variations also appear in the organization of the region and surround. For example, those who provide service may form a nucleus and face clients or customers in the outer zone. But sometimes customers enter the nucleus and areas of refreshment or sale are established in the region.

Intersected, or I, Formations

Ordinarily, strangers and outsiders do not pass through a formation unless the formation blocks a path of public access.

When people in arrays leave a space between them that is large enough for passage and when they do not show their affiliation or involvement, people will pass through.

When aggregates of strangers collect on a beach or in a park, they leave pathways between them so that strangers can cut *between* face formations and gatherings.

In this case there are multiple, separate formations and sites.

In such cases we will say the total aggregate is intersected.

There is yet another case of divided assemblies which is rare in open space, for the divisions in this case are formed by barriers and walls. This situation will concern us in Section III.

Relationships in Complex Formations

The complex formations described in this chapter demarcate multiple zones and/or modules that are separated by rules of occupation, by intersecting pathways, and/or by barriers. So the participants in one part do not exhibit simple unison behavior, involvement, or affiliation relations with those in other sections of the formation. We can, then, add two other kinds of relationships to our coding schema of U, V, W, and X types.

RELATIONSHIPS: TYPE Y

Those in the nucleus of a hub and those in the outer zones are separated by conventions which limit passage. Their relations ordinarily are those of performer and spectator, of salesperson and customer, of professional and client, master and servant, athlete and coach, and so on. These we call "Y" relationships. The behavioral composition of these relationships may not differ in kind from those we have already described in chapters 4 and 5, but the participants do not occupy the same module or zone of space.

RELATIONSHIPS: TYPE Z

If people are separated by a territorial boundary, they may have no relationship at all. But strangers can form visible relationships across a territorial border. In this case we will say they have a "Z" type of relationship in that spatial and territorial context.

_____ TWELVE

territorial fields

We have now sketched out a very broad outline. We have discussed the orientation spaces of an assembled group, as well as the spaces of formations. We should review these constructs and describe how they are used and put together by groups of people as they behave in space and time.

The Territories of Small Clusters

Recall first the spacing of small and simple clusters.

THE SPACE OF AN ELEMENT

An element can consist of one person . . .

or a dyad . . .

or an arc of people.

It can be a row or column . . .

(Photograph by Edward Paul)

or a set of rows and columns.

(Photo by Edward Paul)

      The face formation can have two or a dozen or more members.

The members can occupy but a small module . . .

or a larger area.

They can hold a unified orientation . . .

or form several axes and move apart to form sub-channels

In either event, the space of mutual orientation is called an "o" zone and the total occupied space is called a nucleus.

In a gathering, multiple elements and face formations co-exist.

Any of the relations previously described may occur in each sub-formation at any moment of time.

Sometimes partial relations can be established across the sub-formations.

(Photograph by Edward Paul)

The hub is a combination of solo people, elements, face formations, and/or gatherings in the nucleus. Still other formations occur in the region, or in yet a third zone for spectators.

The zones of the hub are separated by *concentric passage-ways* and rules of territorial defense. In other assemblies of strangers, the separate formations are separated by transecting passages, conventions of non-intrusion, and sometimes by barriers. We call this situation an "intersected formation."

We have named these different formations in such a way that the first letter of each name forms a mnemonic series: e, f, g, h, i. This will help us remember them.

We can thus list them as types of formation, defining each as follows:

e An element (code e) is a row, arc, or file of one or more persons who hold a *common* orientation.

f A face formation (code f) is a section, square, or circle of people who orient *to each other*.

g A gathering (code g) is a cluster of multiple elements and/or face formations in which the participants hold multiple, different orientations but are affiliated and can move from one sub-group to another.

h A hub (code h) is a formation of two or three concentric rows, arcs, or circles of people who face a common nucleus of people, who may in turn face them.

i An intersected formation (code i) is an array of people, engaged in a common activity which is subdivided into separate formations by paths or open spaces.

In Aristotelean thought, we would now have a classification of *types* of clusters. In a systems epistemology, each of these types is *a level of* human clustering more complex than its constituents.

Thus the face formation is an organization of multiple elements: The gathering is an organization of multiple elements and face formations.

The hub is an organization of elements, face formations, and/or gatherings in an inner zone or nucleus which performs in relation to some cluster of formations in one or two outer zones, and so on.

Each of these *levels* may characterize the spatial frame *at various stages* in the activity of an assemblage of people.

These people arrive in elements.

They gather to greet one another.

A few minutes later they will establish another face formation to conduct business. At recess, they will again form a gathering, and so on.

Increments of Space

Each of the three simplest formations will hold or claim three sorts of space:

An "o" space is claimed by the orientations of the participants.

A "p" zone is held for locations and immediate possessions.

An "r" space behind and around this center is respected by passersby and new arrivals.

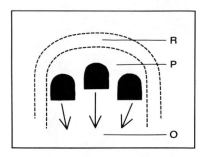

In the case of the elements, these spaces are organized somewhat as follows:

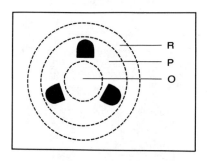

In the case of the face formation, the "o" spaces are combined through mutual involvement and space is organized something like this:

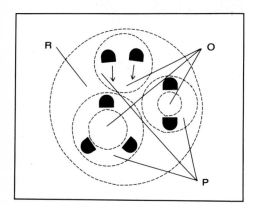

In the case of a gathering, the two configurations just described are combined.

In the case of the hub, an outer zone is defined by its occupation by spectators.

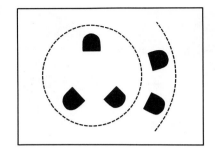

Two status zones may occur exist in the region, a zone of regional associates and a zone of spectators. So the region may be divided into a region and a surround. Concentric passages still exist around the nucleus, and a sixth peripheral zone may be used by passersby and arrivals. All in all, the hub may have as many as six zones:

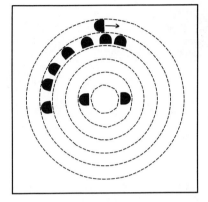

The intersected gathering is transected by pathways that divide it into sections. This sort of multi-site assembly may also have a region, a zone of spectators, and a peripheral zone for transit, service, parking, and so on. Thus the hub and the intersected form can be combined.

For those in the outer zones the entire nucleus is an zone to which they are to orient but not a zone they are to occupy.

To the spectators in the surround the regional associates are within the zones to which they are to orient. But people in the nucleus facing the periphery orient to the outer regions.

Site-Events

As the formations change in time, so do the orientational and occupied spaces.

At one step of the activity, all orientations fix on one focus.

At a next step, the heads and maybe the bodies sweep to another focus.

At one phase of the activity, one kind of relations exist in some sector of the formation.

At another phase, a new configuration of relations forms and other spaces are thereby claimed and respected.

After a number of phases, the participants change locations and orientations and establish a new formation. Then a new stage begins.

The formation changes from this kind . . .

. . . to this kind.

At each stage a different sort of activity begins, and then another is initiated as a new formation is established, and so forth.

The interdependency of site and stage is such that it is artificial to conceptually separate them. Events are sites observed through time and sites are the spatial dimension of events. To develop a space-time construct, we speak of site-events.

A Territorial Field

Now we can imagine a territorial field much as we imagined an orientation field at the end of Chapter 6. Such a field is a customary, ordered pattern of positions, relationships, and clusters.

PART III

BUILT TERRITORIES

We must assume that the behavior we have been describing came to be concretized in the recent course of evolution, for these features characterize furniture groupings of rooms, properties, and larger divisions of fixed human space.

Here in Part III we will describe some of the territorial features of fixed and built spaces. We will begin in Chaper 13 with furniture and furniture clusters. In Chapter 14 we will describe some built areas and domestic rooms. In Chapter 15 we will describe some aspects of property. In Chapter 16 we will take up some features of large fixed territories.

In the main we will describe fixed territories in the British-American tradition, for this culture has been instrumental in shaping built spaces and land divisions in the United States.

_ THIRTEEN

furnishings and set-ups

One way to establish fixed spaces is to use objects that mark a focus of orientation and provide a place to sit down. These furnishings can be arranged in clusters we will call set-ups.

Set-ups provide orientation spaces and spaces for elements, face formations, gatherings and hubs. These clusters are recognized by members of a society who know how to use them and how to assemble within them. A set-up provides a prearranged site and defines what is to occur there.

Objects of Use and Orientation

Spot-sized and cubit-sized objects are placed in the center of a site where they serve as a focus of orientation.

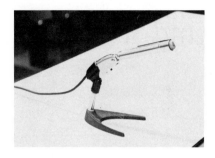

Or they are placed at the ends of a site where they draw orientations and mark the head of the area.

Work surfaces are built and located in such a way that they mark out the modules of space and define the zones of a site.

In centuries past, rugs often defined the orientational space in the center of the living room. Today, small tables are used as well. These range from a cubit to a module in size.

In the meeting area or dining area the whole "o" space is filled with a table that provides eating and work surface and both separates the participants and prevents access throughout the "o" space.

Such built objects appear at the periphery of some spaces. In the kitchen, for instance, the polarity of the area is reversed so that users stand in the "o" space and work at surfaces placed in zones p and q. In other rooms, storage and work spaces are located in the region.

Notice that the built storage spaces are a cubit to a location in size, but these are built together to form a module.

Seats

Locations are also built for seating. These come in cubit and location sizes.

Small modules are also built for sitting and lying down.

Large modules are built by placing multiple rows of seats together.

Some of these are stationary.   Some are placed in vehicles.

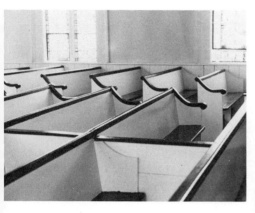

Large elements are also accommodated in multi-modular arrangements of seats that are intersected by aisles.

Formations are more often accommodated by forming clusters of objects and seats. Nuclear formations are usually provided for in this way.

The dining room is a common example. Notice that spot-sized objects such as plates and glasses are clustered in a cubit-sized space in front of each location. A modular-sized table fills the "o" space. Around it in the "p" zone seats are placed. The region is furnished with modules of work space and storage.

In the living room the "o" space is largely open except for low tables. The region is furnished with a cluster of location-sized and modular-sized seats to which are added location-sized pieces to hold lamps and other objects. A writing desk also appears in one section of the region.

A small gathering can also be accommodated by a set-up.

If a sectional sofa is used, it can provide for either a diagonal face formation or for two elements. At the other corner of this room another cluster was arranged for watching television or for conversation.
So two separate face-to-face modules are provided for, but the cluster can be used for a single-face formation too.

(Photograph Courtesy of Edward Paul)

In the restaurant a larger gathering is accommodated. Each table is to be occupied by a small face formation.
In the region are surfaces for varied uses and sometimes tables that accommodate small side-by-side elements.

Set-ups also accommodate hubs of all degrees of complexity. Partial hubs are accommodated by placing a desk or counter in the outer zone of the nucleus. This faces a space or a seat for a visitor in the region.

 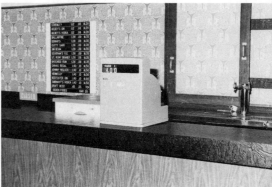

Larger hubs may be established in an auditorium with stage or rostrum at one end and seats for spectators at the other. Or, the full-blown hub can be set up.

IF WE REVIEW WHAT WE HAVE SAID ABOUT SET-UPS, WE CAN ARRIVE AT CERTAIN CONCLUSIONS ABOUT THE COMPOSITION OF OPEN BUT BUILT PLACES.
First of all, any of the components can appear alone.

One can merely set up a location.

Or locations can be clustered to form an element of various sizes.

A V-shaped face-to-face set-up or an L-shaped one can be established. Or a three-, four-, or many-sided nucleus can be set-up.

Such multiple nuclei can be set up with or without intersections.

A nucleus can be set up within or facing a regional element. And one can arrange a section of a hub, a half hub, a full hub, or a circular one.

These outer zones can be sectioned and outfitted with modules and nuclei for providing services, parking, and so on.

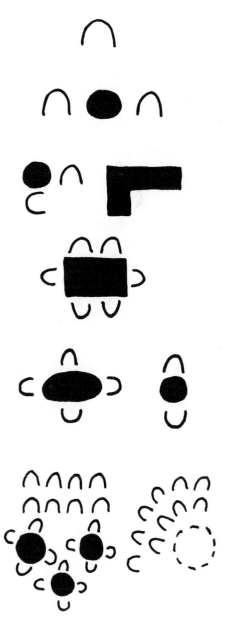

SECOND, WE CAN REPRESENT THE COMPOSITION
OF ANY SET-UP by simple formulas in which we progressively
add elements in sections and zones.

Thus x number of locations forms the simple element and x
number of these forms the compound element in a module.

An x number of arcs or sides form the simple face-to-face
set-up of a nucleus.

An x number of elements and nuclei form the nucleus of a
gathering.

An x number of elements are assembled in a second or regional zone and an x number of elements appear beyond this zone
in the surround for spectators.

So a set-up can be simple or highly complex. In fact, some
consist of multiple gatherings and hubs. And any barriers or combinations of barriers from lines to room dividers can be used to
separate the locations and modules, the sections, and the zones of
the set-up. But for purposes of simplification, we will consider
only four levels of complexity of a set-up.

Level A (area) is a set-up ranging from location size to the size
of a small nucleus and an unoccupied region.

Level B (base) is a multi-area set-up that provides locations
for a nucleus or a set of nuclei and a region that provides for
regional associates.

Level C (compound) provides for a nucleus, a region of people, and a zone of spectators.

Level D is a more complex set-up for multiple gatherings
and/or hubs separated by intersections.

_FOURTEEN

built areas or rooms

Spaces are also marked off by lines, curbs, fences, walls, and other physical structures. Within these spaces, set-ups are located.

At lower levels of organization we find built locations, modules, and areas. These are often rooms. But in a suite or a residence, multiple areas are built together to form a base. And in complex buildings combinations of areas and bases are clustered together. Buildings also have an outer border or perimeter. The total structure is a property.

Marked-Off Spaces

Spaces at various levels often are marked, but they are not closed off by walls. These spaces are portions of larger configurations of built space.

In playing fields, for example, locations or modules may be marked off. Then the court or playing field itself is marked off with lines.

Spectator areas, waiting lines, and paths to various locations may be distinguished by lines or barriers.

Furniture parts and clusters also serve as barriers.

The arms of the chair are an example.

And so are the arms and backs of sofas.

The backs of a circle of chairs or a square of sofas mark the nucleus.

So do the backs of rows of chairs in the surround used by spectators.

By a combination of such spaces, barriers and set-ups, modules, zones, or both modules and zones are established.

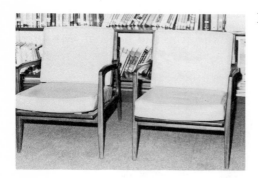

Here, the set-up is a module.

Here it is zoned.

Here it is modular and zoned.

Walls and the Division of Rooms

Notice that up to this point we have described open spaces. These spaces allow people to interact and observe across lines and barriers. *But a set-up can be separated and walled off at any level of organization.*

A location can be walled off.

So can a small module . . .

. . . or a cluster of modules.

A nucleus or small region can be walled off to form an area the size of a room.

A small court can be walled off to form a room.

So can a large one.

A gathering space and its region can be walled off to form a room of the size and complexity of a base.

So can a compound hub, to form a theater or a stadium.

So we can speak of sub-rooms and rooms at level A (area); level B (base); level C (compound); and on rare occasions, level D. The factory is an example.

Notice that there are two general classes of built space, though usually these two kinds appear in combination.

In one kind, the modules and areas are separated by lines or low barriers across which people can see and hear. These built spaces are used for providing service and staging performances.

In the other kind, separate areas or bases are walled off. Persons then cannot see one another. Their spaces are private. In this case, the separate areas and bases have specialized functions. This picture shows the construction of such an arrangement.

It may help us to visualize these arrangements if we review the kinds of spaces that are marked off.

In the center of rooms, "o" spaces are provided for face formations. Into this space people cast their gazes and voices. In the open base or compound, the entire nucleus is a stage or court.

For the central participants, "p" spaces are provided. In face-formation spaces, these participants face the center. In work and service areas, they may face the region. In performance places, the central participants may face either way or move about in the entire nucleus.

At the corners of a face-to-face set-up, we find "q" spaces. They also appear at the rear of the seats in a nucleus so that people can move their chairs back for conversation or for entering and leaving.

REGIONAL SPACES

In some rooms, "r" zones are marked off and hold four modules of objects and spaces for work, toilet facilities, sleep, storage, and passage. In open bases and compounds, the region is marked off for those who support the performance. In separated bases and complexes, the region contains rooms or apartments for the residents.

The "s" zones occupy open places of service and performance for customers and spectators. In walled-off bases and complexes, the "s" zone is used for storage and/or for open grounds.

The participants' spaces we have mentioned so far are stationary ones. Spaces are also provided in which people can move about.

A transit across the "o" space of the nucleus may appear in set-ups like the living room. A "q" space appears between elements to allow people to enter the "o" space or court. In settings around a table, a "q" space appears behind the chairs so that nuclear participants can occupy and leave chairs at the table.

A transit space may also appear between the nucleus and the surround. And "t" spaces may intersect elements of the region and surround. A "t" space lies outside the surround to allow spectators to congregate, avail themselves of services, park belongings, and enter and leave the spectators' zone.

___FIFTEEN

properties

A property is a parcel of land which is built upon, marked off, and owned by a person, a partnership, or an organization.

In a property, one or more rooms are built as a nucleus. The region also may be built up. In a base, the surround is a yard or set of grounds, but this disappears in the urban property. In compound property, the surround is built up as well to provide a third zone of space.

Here we will merely sketch these built spaces. We have described them in detail in another publication.*

---

* Scheflen and Ashcraft (1975).

Built Properties at the Level of Area

The farmer's cottage, and the one-room school and church are properties in which only a single main area was built in the nucleus. Around this main area, a region was fenced off for animals and machinery, or for play, in the case of the school. A surround of farm lands, wooded lots, and other open space appeared at the periphery; and the perimeter of the whole was traditionally marked off by fences, hedgerows, stone walls, or other visible structures.

Properties that Are Bases

The modern residence is a property at the level of a base.

There are usually two nuclear rooms and a central hall in the nucleus of the northern European dwelling, but the central hall has been disappearing in twentieth-century America. In this country the central hall has given way to a residual foyer and a living room and dining room, which are used to receive guests and hold interactions.

Additional rooms appear in the region of the base. In the residential base, the kitchen and the bedrooms are examples. Other regional rooms include pantries, porches, and laundry spaces. In the commercial base, regional rooms appear as offices, storage and filing rooms, washrooms, and so on.

The nucleus and the region of the base have a polarity, or direction of official orientation.

The nucleus of the houses of the ancient Egyptians, Greeks, Romans, Syrians, and Chinese was a central and open court. This arrangement persists today in warm climates. Other rooms faced centrally to this nucleus.

The northern European house and the contemporary house in cooler climates has a covered nucleus on the first story and windows are provided so that these rooms open outward to the region and provide views of any open space at the periphery of the property or beyond its borders.

A property at the level of the base contains zones that are separated from one another by walls. The surround serves as a buffer and a place of storage, though its front may be fixed up for public display. People use a surround but not for working or living purposes. The outer property line lies around the periphery of the surround.

The total base has a zonality. A one-story base is zonal in two dimensions, and a multi-storied base is zonal in three dimensions.

In a full-base, the surround or yard appears on all sides. In the condensed version or row house, the side surrounds have disappeared. The base is then a module of rooms.

The property has yet another zone, at least in theory. *At its outermost perimeter lies a zone or a pair of transits for the passage of strangers.* But this "t" is surrendered by owners to the public domain for alleyways behind the property and sidewalks and streets in front of it.

Complex and Compound Properties

If the surround is built up to provide quarters for spectators, customers, servants, animals, and the like, the property is more complex than a base.

Ancient palaces and the great houses and chateaux of Europe are residential examples. The nucleus consisted of entryways, throne rooms, or great halls. The region contained the chambers and private spaces of the royal family, and the surround provided quarters for slaves, animals, and stored materials. A similar but open example is the stadium, which is also an ancient structure. We will call these one-story, hub-like properties, compounds.

The motel and the hotel are contemporary examples of complex properties, though these structures appear in ancient Greece and Rome as well. The nucleus is a lobby supplemented by meeting rooms, ballrooms and perhaps shops. The region is made up of multiple rooms, suites, or apartments for guests and residents. The surround contains storage areas, maintenance and administrative spaces, and usually grounds and parking facilities. In the hotel and motel, the regional spaces are areas. In the case of the apartment house, each is a base.

Notice that the compound can face centrally as in the college quad or the courtyard palace, or the central space can be enclosed and used for a place of transit, as in the apartment house. These structures can also have a gradient of privacy such that public rooms are in the front near the street whereas private rooms are in the rear.

Multi-Building Divisions

In each of the three levels we have so far described, the nucleus, region and the surround (at level C) are built into a single building or into a main building with some immediately adjacent satellite buildings. But *some properties consist of multiple main buildings, each of which may have its own surround and zone of transit.*

The housing project and shopping center are cases in point.

So are the college campus and the industrial plant.

In sum, we can argue that all properties are at one level of territorial organization that we will call level I: The level of properties. Then we can recapitulate four sublevels as follows:

I.A.—the level of areas
I.B.—the level of bases
I.C.—the level of compounds or complexes
I.D.—the level of multiple divisions.

_____ SIXTEEN

large territories

Among and around properties are interstitial and transit places that are used by the public at large. In addition, large parcels of land may be government-owned. In the United States we can distinguish four such traditional levels, which we will describe in this chapter.

In addition, there are other large territorial divisions, though their boundaries may be rather indefinite and their existence may not be countenanced by laws or even known to the public. Among these are the territories of industrial collectives, the territories of ethnic groups, and the territories of occupational and intellectual movements.

It is usual to cluster properties on city blocks or sections of land.

Between the buildings are alleyways. And between the blocks are sidewalks and streets. These, too are built places, places for transit and congregation.

These transits are open to those who obey the rules of public order.

Along these transits appear the yards (or surrounds) of private properties in rural and residential neighborhoods. But in commercial and governmental districts, the surrounds of properties along the streets and sidewalks are built up. These are semi-public places that can be entered by customers, spectators, and the like, if these people show they belong and conform to the behavioral expectations of the owners.

Land Divisions

Properties lie within larger land divisions. We will designate these divisions as "territories at level II"—the level of land divisions. We can identify sub-levels here, too, and name them as well to maintain a mnemonic schema. In America, levels of land are organized as follows:

Level II.A.
Neighborhoods or
Sections

Level II.B.
Towns, Townships,
Boroughs, and Small Cities

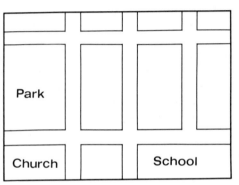

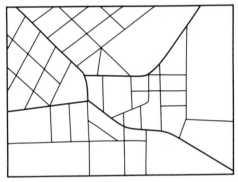

Level II.C.
Counties and Large
Cities

Level II.D
States, Nations, and other
large divisions

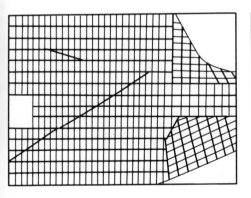

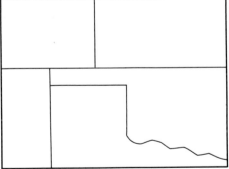

In colonial and Federal America, these land divisions were granted or sold to individuals or groups.

Farmers were often sold one section of land comprising 640 acres, or 1 square mile. At other times in American history, such grants were a quarter section or even a sixteenth section of 40 acres (and a mule).

Nowadays, a section often includes one neighborhood in a city. It has its own wards, voting precincts, health services, and the like, though these are sub-divisions of town or city agencies rather than independent governmental bodies. Thus the section and neighborhood is somewhat analogous to the location in an area and to the area within a property.

In colonial America, town and townships were often granted to privileged individuals or to groups of applicants in parcels from 20 to 40 square miles and sections in area. The grantees laid out these parcels in zones. A village green or square constituted an "o" space at this level. This open space was surrounded by a square of public buildings, much like a "p" zone of an area. The region consisted of dwellings and the surround of open woodlots or farm lands. Today, these units are often municipalities. If urbanized, the surrounds are industrial, park land, or waste land.

The large land divisions, too, are now usually controlled in some measure by county and state governments.

Other Large Territorial Divisions

INSTITUTIONAL DOMAINS

Sometimes a religious institution holds power or influence in a division of land that far exceeds its actual holdings of property. Labor unions and guilds may control services in a large vicinity. So can mobs or crime syndicates. And most important are the domains controlled by large corporations and conglomerates. These organizations not only own large land holdings, but control economic and political affairs within these domains. These domains are now international in scope.

ETHNIC DOMAINS

A particular ethnic group may come to control sections or neighborhoods or blocks of these in the city. A particular ethnic group may also control a county, a state, a nation, or a block of nations. In such cases the customs and values of these people may hold sway in these domains.

TERRITORIES OF IDEAS AND VALUES

Particular ideas, beliefs, and values may spread across institutional and ethnic lines and come to prevail in certain places and land divisions. These systems of ideologies may influence the behavior of all who pass through or inhabit them.

____ PART IV

THE USE
OF
TERRITORIAL FORMS

We have been claiming that human beings have evolved traditional forms of territory that they transmit from generation to generation as a cultural heritage. They employ these forms whenever they come together and they use them again and again to construct buildings and organize tracts of land. As a consequence, they have now marked off most of this planet's surface, some of its waters, and the surface of the moon as well.

We must again stress the field or systems approach in describing such phenomena. Territorial usage at any one level falls under a general system of rights, jurisdictions, and auspices, such that a description of any particular usage falls within a system of contexts at multiple levels.

In the remaining chapters we describe how man uses these territorial forms, and we begin by focusing on routine or ordinary usage. Our comments, of necessity, will be very general, providing only the barest outlines, allowing the reader's experience to fill in the gaps.

SEVENTEEN

the organization
of built space

Before we generalize about how places are used, we must
make a few more broad generalizations about how places are organized. To do this, we abstract those features of territoriality that
apply to any kind of place at any level. Then, we can construct a
paradigm for territorial organization in general, if we note certain
common variations.

Sub-Places at Each Level

We have said that a single location, module, or nucleus may
be walled off and can thus be regarded as a territory in its own
right. But more often, locations, modules, and nuclei are combined, left open to one another, and assigned a region. In these
cases, these areas are but portions of a territory or are sub-places
in a larger places. In residential property, for example, a room
contains about thirty locations. These are organized into several
modules, some of which lie at the center of the whole area. But
the rooms of a house are themselves locations in the dwelling as a
whole. *In fact, we find locations, modules, nuclei, and regions at
all levels of territorial organization.*

LOCATIONS IN AN AREA

To lay the ground work for this generalization, consider again what we have said about locations in an area or room. In Section II we held that each participant is allocated a small space in an assembly. Then in Section III we said that some locations were built as seats or other items of furniture and some were left open at the center, at the corners, and around the outside of an area or room.*

LOCATIONS AT OTHER LEVELS

We can use the term "location" to describe the elemental units of physical space at other levels of territorial organization.

I.B.   The sub-groups of a gathering and the areas and rooms of a base can be considered the locations of the base.

I.C.   At this level the component bases and areas of a compound such as the stadium or a complex such as an apartment house or office building can be considered the locations.

I.D.   The various buildings and complexes of a shopping mall, housing project, a row house development, or an industrial plant can be considered the locations of that division.

We can also generalize the idea of a location to larger units of governmental and institutional turf. Thus:

II.A.   The blocks of a city or suburb constitute the separate locations of a neighborhood.

II.B.   Neighborhoods in the city, small suburban municipalities, and rural villages are locations within the township or small city.

II.C.   Towns, townships, and small cities form the locations within a county, and so on.

Similarly, the separate plants, mines, and other holdings constitute the locations of a corporation. The branches of a union or professional society are its locations, and so on.

---

* We said the "k" space was about four cubic cubits in size. In British-American tradition this size was about (18 × 18 × 18) × 4 English inches. It is now about (24 × 24 × 24) × 4 inches. The location is often about 36 × 36 × 72 inches, or 1 × 4 cubic yards. It is smaller in various settings and in other cultures.

In Section II we used the term "module" to designate a row of locations used by a small element or face formation of dyadic proportions. Then in Section III we described built modules such as the sofa or work counter. Thus an area is set up with one or more modules. We can use the term "module" at all levels.

The base often has a modular form. The row house in eastern America is an example. Each lot has lost its front and back locations to the public domain for streets and alleyways, but six locations remain.* These have a modular form and a form gradient from the street to the rear. This structure can be diagramed as shown at the right.

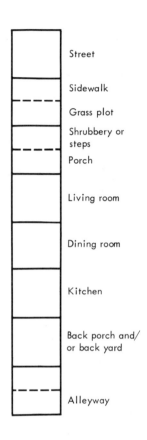

Street

Sidewalk

Grass plot

Shrubbery or steps

Porch

Living room

Dining room

Kitchen

Back porch and/ or back yard

Alleyway

The complex housing building and the compound theatre and shop often have a modular structure. And modules of stores and houses face one another across the streets of a suburb or city.

Modular blocks, neighborhoods, and towns are sometimes found along railroads, rivers or waterfronts, but the module is not the usual form of large land division.

---

* In the British-American tradition, each of the locations is classically a square (British) rod, (i.e., 15 × 18 feet). Thus the modular lot is 1 by 8 rods, or 2 English chains in length.

In Section II we described nuclear clusters of locations and modules in the face formation or at the center of a hub. Then in Section III we described the table-chair nucleus of dining and meeting rooms and the open-court nucleus of conversational rooms such as the living room and of work rooms like the kitchen. Now we can argue that nuclear formations occur at any level of territorial organization.

I.B.   One can find an analogous nucleus at the level of the base. In the classical Mediterranean, Chinese, and West African house, the nucleus was an open court. In the traditional North European house, it was a great hall or more recently two interaction and entertainment rooms and a central hall.

One can also identify a nucleus in many neighborhoods. In ancient times it was an *agora* or marketplace. Nowadays, it is often a small square. A monument or open space lies at the center as an "o" zone. This zone is surrounded by a "p"-like zone of public buildings and stores. Towns and cities exhibit analogous nuclei. Counties have county seats, etc.

The Paradigm of a Total Unit

MULTI-NUCLEI AND REGIONS

It is quite common at all levels of organization for a territorial unit to have multiple nuclei and thus to accommodate a gathering. We find this arrangement in open space and in some rooms. The base and complex often have halls and lobbies and several meeting and eating spaces. Neighborhoods, towns, and cities, too, have multiple nuclei for shopping, commerce, entertainment, government, and so on.

And each site and built territory has a region, as we have repeatedly described. This region may be anything from a token space to a place with multiple rooms, suites, houses, blocks, and neighborhoods; and it is likely to have as many as three sub-zones—region, surround, and zone of transit.

THE COMMON PARADIGM

At any level of organization, then, there are structures of six zones that can be diagramed schematically.

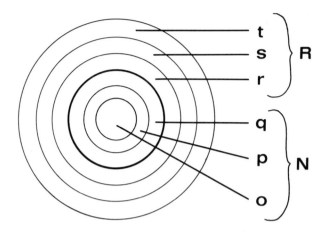

Major Variants

Certain major variants of this schema appear again and again in assemblies of people and in the organization of their built spaces.

1. Sometimes only one location, one module, or less than six zones may be walled off and appear as a property or land division in its own right.

2. The polarity of the entire unit of territory may be centripetal or centrifugal. Thus the people of status may occupy the center and a gradient of decreasing status proceeds outward zone by zone. Or the opposite arrangement may occur. If a single module is built, then the gradient proceeds from one end to the other as if the head end represented the nucleus of the total form. Furthermore, the polarity and gradient of the unit may occur in three dimensions by using raised areas or stories.

3. The spaces may be left open or walled off for private and specialized usage.

4. Any locations or modules in any or in all zones may be replicated again and again to form multiple units of similar status and function. Thus there may be many bedrooms, many apartments, many residential blocks, and so on.

We can regard this organization as species-specific for contemporary man since it appears in all cultures in one form or another. This does not mean that the paradigm is inherited or passed down in the genes.

Here is the point of all this. *These divisions of fixed territory lie within one another like Chinese boxes.* And each is a seat of certain mores, customs, rules, laws, and agencies of enforcement, for the land divisions are the holdings of governments.

Each event occurs in an area that lies within a base, that lies within a neighborhood, that lies within a borough or town, and so on. At each of these levels there are systems of regulation, such as laws, mores, economic regulations, and subcultural traditions. *So any human event falls under the aegis and influence of a system of successively larger systems.* To take the point to its extreme, any act in any location is in some degree influenced by the organization of behaviors and things within that area. The organization of activities and spaces in an area in turn depends on the organization of the base, and so on.

The interdependence of levels also extends in the other direction. Behavior at any level is influenced by the component actions in the component spaces.

Thus the contexts of any space or event are organizations of behavior at successive levels of property and land divisions. But the matter of contexts is more complicated than this. As we shall see, there are other divisions of territorial behavior. For example, ethnic peoples have migrated through many land divisions and their customs may appear in any property or neighborhood, for they are carried there by the people who grew up in these cultures. Contexts are thus represented within us.

__EIGHTEEN

site-occasions

Within built territories, people carry out solitary and group activities. In doing so they establish territorial sites and hold them for a while in accordance with traditional programs and schedules of activity.

The Programming of Site Forms

In any activity the participants will employ some series of points, spots, and links, as we have described in Section I. In a physical task, for instance, the participants may lay hold of one object or tool after another. In a conversational type of activity, they may look one way and then another and form and break tactile and other links in accordance with the steps and phases of that particular form of activity.

We can make the same generalization about orientations and relations. The participants in a physical task may turn from one operation to the next, and in meeting they may jointly address one speaker then another one. In doing so, certain members of the group co-act while others are involved or affiliated and still others watch. Then this pattern of allegiances and involvements may shift in accordance with the agenda of the event. And similarly, the formations of the assembly will change from stage to stage until the participants leave the scene altogether.

On a particular occasion, a particular kind of place will usually be used for a particular kind of activity. The layout and decor of the place will signal what is supposed to occur there. So will the location of the place and the occasion. But the nature of the place will also limit and constrain what can go on. *There is an important relation between the nature of the place—i.e., the setting—and what can go on there.* Similarly, the local conditions will influence the site and the progress of the event. Thus density, temperature, noise level, and other conditions shape a site event.

Schedules and Occasional Events

Just as the program of a customary activity shapes its phases and stages, so the scheduling of place governs the uses of that place. In the simplest case, a given kind of place has been built and set up for a particular kind of activity. A place such as this is used only on particular occasions. The stove, the dining room, the chapel, the stadium, and the town park are examples.

But this relationship between occasion and special place holds only for formal and official activities. In this dimension of place-use, the built territory is used in accordance with a fixed and traditional schedule. But even special places are used when unusual contingencies occur. Stoves are used for purposes other than preparing formal meals. The dining room may be used for card-playing and preparing income tax returns. The church is employed for meetings when a crisis develops that concerns the congregation. So we can distinguish routine and customary occasions and emergent and contingent ones in the scheduling of place.

In addition, any place is used between occasions for maintenance activities. Even a special place must be cleaned, repaired or rebuilt. And the administrative members of any social group may meet to decide policy, administer discipline, plan fund-raising campaigns, and so on. Furthermore, all places are used for hanky-panky of various kinds. All in all, then, we must recognize the inter-occasional use of even the most special and occasional place.

The Use of Multi-Site Places

Some places are built and used for a particular kind of activity, but they may be used sequentially by different people for a variety of occasions. This generalization, too, can be made at each level of territorial organization.

For example, a spot on a person's body may be used for display at one phase of an activity and for tactile contact at another. And the people who are allowed to observe the display may not be permitted by rules of etiquette and affiliation to touch that body spot. Similarly, a location may be used for sitting but it may be used by one person after another. One person may doze in this location while another uses it for reading and a third converses with another person while occupying the location. The kitchen may be used by the mother to prepare food and then by several household members to eat it. Still later the same area is used for conversation and drinking, and so on. And the large room or base may be used for one wedding and one bar mitzvah after another. In fact, a transit place may be used continuously by one group after another around the clock. In the morning it is used by people enroute to work. Later in the morning it is used by tradesmen and shoppers, and so on.

Once again, we should take heed of a relationship between routine and contingent usage. Although a given place may be used officially and customarily for one kind of site and then another in the course of everyday events, it may be used for any reason at all under conditions of crisis, disruption, or secrecy.

Places like these are used for one site-event after another according to some customary scheduling. But there are also places that are ordinarily used for multiple, *simultaneous,* site-events. The living room is a case in point. It may be used for homework on one occasion, television-watching on another and entertaining on still another. *But it may be used for all of these activities at one and the same time,* as it characteristically is in the crowded working-class apartment in the city. To make such uses of a place, gatherings of separate sites are established in different modules or nuclei by separate set-ups of furniture or by separate systems of orientation.

Multiple-simultaneous use of place can also be identified at all levels of territorial organization. Just as the locations in an area can be used in different ways, so can the different spots on a person's body and the spots on a table. And at the other extreme we can observe that the locations within a building and those within a neighborhood or city can be used for very different kinds of site-events at the same time. In New York City, for example, there are whole neighborhoods built and used for theater-going, for the work of furriers, for sale of electrical equipment, jewelry, and so on.

If a place is being used for a single activity, that activity will have a site and program that is traditional for that place in a particular system of traditional aegis. This aegis will be institutional, regional, and cultural. When a place affords space to multiple, diverse site-events, each of these may have a different aegis. Special conventions of co-allowance and co-existence have evolved to make this possible.

NINETEEN

holdings and jurisdictions

Some people can occupy and control some portion of territory for some period of time. This right of occupation depends on their conformity to the rules of occasion and aegis and on their acceptability to those who have jurisdiction at a higher level of organization.

Holdings for an Occasion

During some phases of an activity the participants can rest their possessions, hands, and eyes on certain spots. But these spots may change from phase to phase. Similarly, participants in an activity have rights at certain phases to take a particular orientation. They can address a particular place and sometimes project their voices to it.

The holdings of a location can also be specific to a particular stage of a site-event. Thus a candidate may be allowed to take part in a meeting only when certain subjects are under discussion. A child may join the adults at only certain stages of the family outing. Similarly formations may appear at one stage of the event and be disbanded at others. In a game, for instance, the contestants may line up in stationary formation, run a play, and then line up again.

So participants may be expected and allowed to occupy certain locations in certain formations for certain intervals. They may also be restricted to certain modules in a set-up. Members of one faction may be required to sit on one side of the table, for instance. Furthermore, people of given role and status may be restricted to certain zones within an area. And given rooms may be rented or loaned only for an occasion, so the members have rights to that room or building only for a certain period of time.

We can generalize the idea of holdings to even higher levels of territorial organization. Members of certain ethnic groups may stay in a certain neighborhood for a few decades or so and then move on.

More Lasting Rights to Remain

The right to lay claim to an area of space and the right to use it for an occasion are rights of relatively short duration. People may stay longer in a place if they have tenants' rights or rights of ownership.

Workers in a corporation or an institution are a case in point. These people may have a workbench or desk of their own and rights to the washroom and cafeteria as long as they are employed there. These rights are occasional insofar as they apply only during the working day, but they are rights of tenancy in that they can apply five days a week for months or years.

In residential property, rights of tenancy may be granted by the owners to their children, pets, and relatives. In the urban apartment the poor child may have rights of tenancy to part of one closet, to one bed, to one chair in the dining area, and occasional rights to one living room chair. On the other hand, the entire household may stay in a house or apartment by rights of tenancy granted by an agency or owner.

The members of an institution may also be given rights of tenancy by the institution. Thus the mental patient gets one bedside table and occasional rights to his bed during the night and to one day-room chair during the day. But some members are given tenancy to offices and to living quarters in the institution.

Similarly, a people may be granted rights of tenancy to a neighborhood or town, but such rights are often taken without any formal grant.

Under certain conditions people are given rights to occupy and use a place for an indefinite length of time. They can obtain these rights by grant or purchase. Once having obtained such rights, owners can grant tenancy to others. But even owners must yield territory to the public domain and entire properties may be condemned in the public interest. Ownership is also yielded at all levels by conquest.

In sum, we can distinguish five levels of occupational rights, as follows:

Claims are behaviors that are employed to gain control of a territory.

Occasional Uses are granted to persons in certain roles and memberships for the duration of a stage or event.

Tenancy is granted to certain persons for longer periods of time if they supply certain services, pay fees, and/or obey the rules of usage.

Ownership is granted to those who buy or build a place.

Rights of conquest and condemnation, however, can be exercised at higher levels of organization.

Notice that spaces can be obtained, held, and controlled at each of the levels of territorial organization that we have described in this book—i.e., at levels from spot to state. And each holding occurs at some level of temporal control from claim to conquest.

Jurisdiction

Those who occupy a territory at any level have some jurisdiction in that space-time unit. They have control over those who are granted less durable rights, for example. Owners can force the eviction of tenants and tenants can cause a visitor to be removed. And anyone with occasional rights to a place can reject the claims of others.

Those who have jurisdiction in a place also have some responsibilities. They are not to violate the territorial rights of those within their jurisdiction. Thus the government is not supposed to invade the private property of citizens; owners are not to enter the apartments of tenants except in an emergency; parents are not supposed to enter the bedrooms of teen-age daughters except to discipline them and clean the room, and so on. Furthermore, those who hold space have an obligation to the hierarchy of traditional aegis. If they do not use the space allocated to them in accordance with these rules of custom and tradition, they may be displaced.

Yet each jurisdiction is itself under a larger jurisdiction. Thus the resident falls under the jurisdiction of multiple levels of government from municipality to nation. And governments fall under the jurisdiction of multi-national corporations. So jurisdiction is usually invested at higher and higher levels of territorial organization, just as it is usually invested at longer and longer levels of tenure.

___ TWENTY

access and mobility

We have said that people have rights to act in and occupy space for a certain period of time. Correspondingly, they have certain rights of access and mobility into and through fixed territories. Just as their rights to act and remain are constrained at higher levels of organization, so are their rights to move about so restricted.

Rights to Relationship

Rules govern the rights of people to access to other people and to the sites other people have established. We can codify these rights by using the mnemonic set we described in Section I.

X rights. People in public places have the right to be co-present but they have little or no rights to one another unless they can demonstrate an extraordinary need or claim a common membership or affiliation. Thus they take "X" types of relationship.

U rights. People who are oriented in common have rights to co-act, but they do not have the right to mutual involvement unless they can establish something else in common.

V rights. But those who share a zone, an acquaintanceship, or a membership in an activity can become involved and thus establish a face formation and a site.

W rights.   Those who have been involved may establish a sanctioned and lasting social relationship. Then they have rights to be together and to go together.

Y rights.   Those who are admitted to the region of a site or place may have supportive or observers' rights to those in the nucleus.

Z rights.   But persons outside a territory have no rights to those inside unless a previous affiliation exists among them or unless those outside have a reasonable claim to admission.

Mobility Within a Zone

When a person claims and is granted the right to occupy a location in an area, he can shift about in that location as space permits. He does not, however, have automatic rights to gaze into and reach into other and adjacent locations. He may gaze into the "o" space of the site or set-up and in fact is expected to do so during a performance. And he may peer into the locations of those with whom he is involved, or affiliated. But this person is not supposed to stare at just anyone.

Similarly, rights to a location in an area do not per se give rights to move about the whole area. For example, one may be allowed to occupy a side location, but not a head location. And rarely do visitors or guests have a right to poke into storage locations in the region of an area. In addition, there may be items in some locations of an area that are off limits to all but the owners. One must *ask* to use the telephone, for instance.

Rules like this apply at all levels of territorial formation. For example, a spectator may use the seats of the surround, the toilet and refreshment facilities that are built into the surround, and the parking facilities of the "t" zone, but not move from one seat in the theater or stadium to another. Those who belong to alien cultures and classes will be discouraged from entering certain shops, offices, and government buildings.

We could use the code letters "L" and "M" to describe rights to locations and modules in a zone. We can use the code letters for zones to describe zonal rights as follows:

T rights.   Non-participants have a right to pass by and sometimes through a territory provided they behave in certain ways and do not force an entry.

S rights. Peripheral participants have rights to watch certain performances or enter to buy something or avail themselves of other services.

R rights. People who will play a supportive or regulatory role in an activity can enter the region around the nucleus and in some set-ups they can enter the nucleus.

P rights. Regional and even nonparticipants can pass through a nucleus but those who remain in the nucleus there are main or central participants.

O rights. In moving activities, main participants can enter the zone "o." In stationary ones, they use this space for orientations and involvements.

We must remember that all rights of access and mobility are relative. They are relative to role and activity, existing relationships, and memberships in institutions, and they are relative to class, region, and ethnic tradition.

Paths of Transit

The room of the base or complex may permit passage through or around the nucleus and provide visible transits for such movement ("o" space and "q" zone transits). And we have said that all properties and land divisions have transit zones at their periphery. These, too, are built as alleyways, sidewalks, streets, and highways.

In addition, land divisions are often transected by public transportation. Railroads, buslines, and subway tunnels are examples. Today there are also lanes of transit in the air space above properties and land divisions.

Notice that what are nuclear transits at one level of organization are peripheral or "t" zones at the next level. For example, the transits through the center of a neighborhood or town are "t" zones between the blocks of that neighborhood, and what are alleyways *through* a block are peripheral "t" spaces of each house or building on that block. Thus the designation of a transit is relative to the level of territorial organization. As a consequence, one who is passing through the open streets of a neighborhood is passing by the private property of a person or corporation. One who is passing through the open corridors of a building is passing by the separate office suites of the tenants. *Thus, one must obey several rules of passage at the same time.*

TWENTY-ONE

territorial regulation

There are a variety of forms of behavior that maintain and regulate the stability of territorial forms. These include signs, cues, monitors, disciplinary actions, "gating" mechanisms, and territorial defense. But each member of a culture holds a cognitive image of territorial form and thus uses these forms in customary ways and replicates them over and over. In these ways customary forms and hierarchies are maintained. These behaviors can also be used to modify and change territorial forms.

Behaviors that Maintain Territorial Form

We have repeatedly mentioned that a territorial form constitutes a gestalt that experienced members of a tradition can recognize. Hence they can know immediately where to go and what to do there.

CUES AND SIGNS

If there is any ambiguity about the matter, a traveler can ask directions or follow a program or a guide book. In addition, signs and symbolic codes of color and design indicate the kind of place and the transits that pass through it.

MONITORS AND DISCIPLINARY ACTIONS

If one offends the territorial rules of a place, he may elicit scowls, sneers, juts, frowns, and other kinesic monitors that indicate a transgression. If he is not forewarned by these signals, he may be verbally called down, scolded, warned, or instructed. There are, of course, more drastic forms of punishment for territorial offenses. And one who repeatedly offends may be reindoctrinated in the social rules.

SYNCHRONY

When people share a common experience, site, place, or occasion they may automatically walk, move, hold and otherwise behave in the same temporal rhythms. In such cases each participant's behavior maintains and regulates the behavior of the others.

GATING

There are conventions that restrict the usurpation of adjacent locations and modules and the crossing of zones within an open site. These conventions are known to socialized members of any culture and they are enforced by the behavior of those already assembled. Frowns, scowls, reprimands, and challenges are means of enforcing such conventions.

In built places, locations, modules, and territorial divisions are marked off, for instance, by fences and walls. Thus locations, modules, and zones can be entered only at certain points of entry and exit. These points of passage are protected by physical mechanisms such as gates and doors and by conventions of passage.

When people have rights of entry, they must display these in some way to those who bear the task of surveillance. Members and guards may negotiate an entry by an exchange of recognition signals or by a display of the badges and clothing of membership and a head nod of acknowledgement.

By the same token, most people know how to show that they are merely passing through, so they do not challenge gating of most places. They wear certain clothing and obey certain rules of deportment. They drop their gaze, dip their head slightly, curl their shoulders, and keep their hands close to and in front of their bodies.

COGNITIVE IMAGES

All members of common culture must carry cognitive images of the shape of familiar territories. We can observe this phenomenon by watching them move about in familiar places in an expected manner.

In some degree all people can represent space layouts by gesticulating, drawing or sketching, giving oral directions, and the like. And some members draw blueprints of territorial layouts building familiar kinds of space over and over again. In fact, the members of a culture replicate customary forms century in and century out across states, nations, and continents. The rod-sized room can be traced back to ancient Egypt and to pre-Aztec civilizations, and the English chain (66 English feet) was used as a measuring device in ancient civilizations as well as today.*

CONCEPTIONS AND AFFECTS

Most people are not necessarily conscious of territorial matters. But they do feel anxious when their territories are violated and often become very angry. In fact, we can argue that hostility results from territorial threat. Similarly, people may fill a gap in their conscious territorial knowledge with all sorts of notions and myths. These are often fostered by academic and political figures (see Chapter 24).

A conscious knowledge of territorial forms and a set of generalizations about multiple territorial forms can be regarded as a "meta-territorial" activity. Such knowledge allows us to describe, modify, and manipulate territorial forms and to use or abuse them.

---

* The rod has been a variable measure. The classical British rod is 16.5 feet.

PART V

TERRITORIAL DISTURBANCE

In Part IV we sketched some of the routine uses of territorial form. These routine uses come into play when the setting is of traditional size and form, is not very crowded, and when the jurisdiction and aegis of an event is unambiguous at all levels of organization. Uncomplicated cases like this are often found in rural and suburban areas where the people are of similar background.

The territoriality of crowded and heterogeneous places is not so simple. In the city, for example, places have become smaller while population has increased. All sorts of liberties have been taken with the territorial forms of a people in order to save money and maintain the turf of majority peoples against the invasion of alien and poorer populations. Places built by one people are used by another and many traditions try to share the same properties and neighborhoods. As a result, the customary territoriality of places and sites is disturbed.

TWENTY-TWO

uncustomary territorial forms

Often we find ourselves in situations where something is amiss. We are likely then to search our ideas and look about us to identify the problem and explain it. Each of us has his favorite kind of explanation. Some favor psychological explanations. Some lean to physiological ones. Others favor social or economic explanations.

If we have a spatial-temporal frame of reference, we may be able to recognize that the territorial behaviors we observe are not traditional or customary. But it will do little good to simply add another diagnostic word to our list of semantic notions. There are complex kinds of uncustomary behavior that warrant our examination.

Unfamiliar Forms

A person or a group of people may regard certain uses of space as strange or deviant simply *because they are unfamiliar*.

For example, urbanites tend to use social distance and conventions of mutual avoidance in crowded public places. To rural Americans, this behavior suggests an unfathomable lack of human concern and responsibility. Urbanites view with suspicion the fact that rural Americans know one another's business and take responsibility for one another's children.

The lower classes have long regarded middle-class residential space as a matter of conspicuous consumption, whereas middle-class Americans consider the residential and neighborhood crowding of poor urban peoples are some sort of immorality stemming from a lack of ambition and decency.

The Latin and the Eastern-European Jew regard the British and British-American tendency to hold large locations and maintain strict conventions of privacy as a sign of coldness and detachment. When, on the other hand, a middle-class American observes the tendency of Puerto Rican family members to huddle together and stroke one another by the hours, he is likely to turn green with envy or postulate some severe incestuous or oedipal problem.

Cross-regional, cross-class, and cross-ethnic territorial experience can sometimes make us aware that behavior can be different without being pathological. Then we are not forced to be redneck conservatives or pseudo-indulgent liberals. We can examine the contexts of territorial behavior instead.

Territorial Accommodation

Space usage can be uncustomary because the uses must accommodate to distortions in a territorial hierarchy.

A place may be too small for the activities it is to accommodate and/or for the number of users and occupants, or it may have been subdivided so that its gradient or zonality is distorted. Then people do not know how they are to use it, though they often accommodate to the situation somehow. One can describe unusual places at all levels of the territorial hierarchy, from huge and strangely shaped chairs to pentagonal or round buildings and indeed to neighborhoods chopped up by railroads, elevated trains, rivers, and expressways.

It may also be that a place is familiar enough in size and layout but that unusual noise, lighting, heating, and crowding prevail there for a while and interfere with work and communication, with ownership and control, or with mobility and regulation.

A place and its environmental conditions may be stable and customary, but it presents difficulties, nevertheless, because it poses a confusing or distorted jurisdictional or aegis problem. It may be, for instance, that a familiar place is taken over by another people or another jurisdiction, so it is not clear what activity is to be conducted there and under what mores, customs or rules. Invariably the victors will constrain the vanquished. The original inhabitants are not permitted to assume their usual positions or they maintain but token jurisdiction. They cannot move into or out of their old spaces. The ghetto is a familiar example.

Territorial Manipulation

Animals who are overcrowded in spaces that are lacking in resources tend to move and migrate. People usurp other people's locations and invade adjacent properties, neighborhoods, and cities, and countries. Those victimized by territorial usurpation may denounce the invaders as simply savage and barbaric, but population density, the shortage of food and other resources also play a role in small and in large migrations and invasions. There are additional considerations as well. For example, since territorial ownership is a mark of status and power, man may manipulate the possession of space on this basis, too.

So humans plan strategic ways to control and acquire territory and one can observe tactics in the service of such plans at all levels of organization. At the smallest space-time segments, one can observe a participant gradually acquire rights to speak by looking to one listener after another until he has recruited an audience. One can observe the subtle use of elbows in a crowded group, a use that gives little excuse for conscious complaint, yet results in a larger and larger location. Similarly, properties, neighborhoods, and nations are acquired.

Deviant Territorial Behavior

There are people who behave strangely even by the criteria of their own regional, class, and ethnic backgrounds, and even when there is no *evident* disturbance of territorial form.

The people we consider deviant habitually exhibit unusual pointing and orientation behavior, unusual location behavior, and/or unusual behavior of mobility and gating. We cannot describe these matters in detail here because of space limitations, but we can offer examples at each level of organization.

Unusual link and orientational behavior. Some people habitually touch spots on the bodies of other people with whom they have not established tactile rights. These same people may avoid touching and looking at those whom they are allowed to contact. Some persons adjust their eyes to spots behind those with whom they are involved. They project their voices beyond those who are listening to them or else they under-project and talk to the floor. They orient away from their partners, be it in conversation or courtship. In fact such people may refuse or avoid affiliations with anyone other than their kinfolk for a life-time.

Deviancy of locations and zone. Part of the behavior we consider deviant involves an unusual use of locations and zones. Some people force their way into locations that obviously belong to people of ownership or authority while avoiding the locations assigned to them. Or, they take locations and roles usually assigned to persons of another gender or another age group.

Similarly, there are persons who always push into the nucleus of any activity even though they are supposed to fill regional or spectator locations. As they do so, they sit and stand so close as to violate all the criteria governing that relation in that event in that culture. Other individuals, on the other hand, are always found in the region or surround when they are expected to play a nuclear role. We can generalize this point to all levels. For example, just as there are persons who stay in the peripheral zones of rooms and properties, so there are people who spend their lives in the outlying zones, the interstices of neighborhoods, towns and cities.

Unusual mobility behaviors. Some people walk across the thresholds of other people's territories without even pausing for a glance of recognition. Still others hang back at thresholds they are expected to cross. Here, too, we can generalize this idea to the thresholds of territories at all levels. Some people not only break into rooms without having rights to do so, but also break into private properties at all levels. And some people lead invasions of neighborhoods, cities, and nations.

Similarly, there are people who slink furtively through transit zones to which they have every right, while others swagger through the sites of other people and through their properties and enclaves.

Uncustomary and deviant territorial behaviors can be studied in a systematic way. The standards for a given kind of space in a given system of contexts can be determined by direct observation. Then non-traditional uses can be studied at all levels of territorial organization. But uncustomary use at any one level must be examined in the context of the total hierarchy before it can be explained or judged.

TWENTY-THREE

distortions of place

If we search about us to find an explanation for an uncustomary territorial form, the first thing we will discover is the place. In fact, distortions of place are the best-known examples of unfamiliar and disrupted territorial behaviors. Increased density and crowding are the most common of all. So we shall say something about crowding in this chapter, but we will see that crowding is a complex relation in itself and that it is but one form of place distortion.

Decreasing Living Space

Throughout history less living space has been accorded to the poor and urbanites than has been allocated to the wealthy and to suburbanites. In urban Egypt the bedrooms in slaves' quarters were as small as 4 × 6 English feet in area, and the ghetto apartment today is about 2 square rods (about 540 square feet) in total area.* The villas of wealthy ancients, however, were huge in area and the middle-class suburbanite in contemporary America enjoys a living space of about 8 square rods, a storage space at least twice this area, and yard space to boot.

The living space available to people of various classes and vicinities has been remarkably constant from ancient times until

---

* Scheflen and Ashcraft (1975).

very recently. The working family in Amarna and Thebes lived in four 1-rod rooms on the ground floor just as does the working-man in his row house in northeastern American cities. The Greek villa was comparable in size to the suburban middle-class house today. And apartments built in Manhattan for the well-to-do in the late nineteenth century consisted of six 1-rod rooms.† But since about 1900 the allocation of living space has decreased in the American Northeast for well-to-do and poor and for urbanites and suburbanites alike. This process continues. Mean living space is less now than it was in the 1950s.**

To some extent this decrease is consonant with the fact that the average American household is smaller today than it was in the early 1900s. But the households of some minority groups who now live in our eastern cities are not smaller. So in some regions of the U.S. living space has decreased without a concomitant decrease in the number of inhabitants.

This decrease in the size of the base has been accomplished by several methods of engineering. First of all, the surround is left off by placing the residence in rows and later by placing apartment units in a compound. With the row house, the side surround is lost. With the apartment house, all yards and grounds disappear (for individual households) and the attic and basement areas, too, are lost. In addition, part of the region is sacrificed in packed and stacked housing. The spare bedroom disappears. So does the work shop and laundry area. Notice, however, that this practice appeared in ancient Thebes, Athens, and Rome and is not characteristically modern.

A second technique for decreasing living space is condensation of the nucleus. It is characteristic, for instance, to combine the kitchen and the dining area, or to combine the living and dining room, into one room, and to omit the central hall.

Finally, the size of each remaining area has itself been reduced. Except in tenement housing, the traditional main rooms of the house and apartment were 1 square rod in area in British-American housing units about 1920. These areas are now about nuclear size—i.e., about 9 × 12, or slightly larger.

Crowding

In the contemporary city another practice, often illegal, has resulted in an increase in density. The traditional apartment of

---

† Ibid.
** Ibid.

the 1930s, which had about six rooms, *has been further subdivided to form two or even three smaller apartment units.* These are often about two rooms in area, and the increased number of units per apartment house has also increased the density of population per city block.

The practice of stacking and packing units to form the apartment house and the high rise has also served to reduce living space and increased population density at the level of neighborhoods and sections of the city. The open surrounds of the nineteenth century have been replaced by gridiron residential blocks and industrial compounds, and the large apartment buildings in the region of the neighborhood contain many more families per city block. In the nineteenth century the urban residential block in eastern seaboard cities housed about 128 households per city block. (Each lot covered about 8 rods, minus streets). The contemporary tenement with subdivided apartments houses as many as 500 households and the high-rise may increase this figure geometrically.

In sum, the increase in housing units per block and the tendency to build housing in all zones of the neighborhood increases the population density per room or rod, per base or chain, per property, per block, and per section. (Urban planners must sooner or later realize that urban land is not measured in acres. It is measured in rods, chains, blocks, and sections.)

Incomplete Places

When a place has been subdivided, it may be missing some of its usual components. In this case the remaining spaces may become crowded or they may have to be used for activities that are customarily carried out in another place. Thus, the place may be crowded with overlapping activities as well as too many people. *In fact, the ultimate criterion of crowding must be the opportunity to carry out usual tasks and functions, not just the number of occupants.*

Similar problems of place arise when a place is incompletely constructed. Some of its usual locations may be omitted, for example, to save money. Or the nucleus may be insufficient in size or in subdivisions for a particular kind of activity because the planner did not understand that sort of event in that particular tradition. Or the region and surround may be left off to save space. In one notorious building in Philadelphia the architects and builders alike forgot to include the staircases. In such places activities must be given up or combined with other activities.

Unterritorial Places

Some places are planned and built in accordance with a consideration other than territorial organization. They are built to represent God, for instance, or to conform to some aesthetic notion of the human body. The functional dimensions of place are neglected. We can call such places "unterritorial" in the relative sense. They do not follow traditional territorial forms, but territorial behaviors must and do occur within them. The Pentagon is an example; so is the radial, octagonal church.

Ambiguous and Indefensible Places

The omission of portions of places may produce another territorial problem. The boundaries of private places may become less clearcut, and less defensible.*

Two practices in urban planning and building bring outsiders into the very heart of residential turf. These are loss of the surround and the location of transits such as lobbies, elevators, and corridors in the nucleus of the complex. Even in housing projects that retain surrounding grounds it is unlawful to close them to the general public if federal money was used to finance the project. Thus the time-honored pattern of concentric zones with greater privacy and protection at the nucleus has disappeared.

Furthermore, as Newman points out, there is a tendency to omit the traditional markers of zones at the outside of the property.* The corridors of the building open directly onto the street without so much as a token fence, a canopy, a marked off area outside the door, or any other indication of transition from public to private turf. In poorer sections of the city the doorman and concierge are no longer present at the gate.

Newman presents overwhelming statistical evidence that violence rises alarmingly in direct relation to the absence of these outer zones and markers and with the absence of surveillance. This increase occurred independent of class or color, so we can no longer blame urban violence in residential districts on the color or social class of the residents.

---

* Newman (1972).

TWENTY-FOUR

incongruities in the hierarchy

We can thus blame certain distortions in the use of space and time on the place in which the activities are held. But there is more to the matter. The place may be quite traditional and satisfactory in conventional terms, but there may be an ambiguity about the jurisdiction and aegis of the event. This ambiguity may stem from the fact that a heterogeneous group of people are using it and/or from the fact that rights and constraints at one level of territoriality are not in accordance with those at other levels.

Actually, these mixed and incongruent relations not only may explain territorial disturbances in an accustomed place but may also explain distortions in the place itself.

Heterogeneity Among Users

When people share a common tradition, they understand the markers of zones and modules and the signs of direction and gating. But when people of many backgrounds use the same places, they do not necessarily understand one another's territorial codes. Nor do they share in common the same conventions of territorial passage and respect.

We can observe examples of this sort of territorial ambiguity and misunderstanding at all levels of territorial organization. What is considered the usual right to touch in Eastern European

Jewish or Puerto Rican cultures are considered territorial violations in the British-American and Black American cultures. What are usual interpersonal distances in Spanish-American cultures are spatial violations in large-space-using cultures such as the Black American and Northern European American cultures. Staring into an assembled face formation is characteristic among Italian-Americans and Germans. It is an affront in other cultures. In old ethnic neighborhoods the resident of a row house believes he owns and is responsible for the sidewalk and parking space in front of the house, but this right is not respected by other peoples. And the resident of an old ethnic neighborhood who once felt responsible to keep the street under surveillance and report violence closes the drapes and shrugs his shoulders at incidents that would concern people of other ethnic backgrounds.

Incongruity of Jurisdiction and Aegis

Territorial order depends on the observance of some particular tradition of behavior—a tradition maintained at all levels by a system of aegis. This system is, in turn, enforced by a hierarchy of jurisdiction. If there is confusion about which traditional system of rules obtains and/or if there is a mixed or incompatible system of jurisdiction, the territorial order may be correspondingly confused and disrupted.

Here is an example. A harmonious use of the rules of passage in a public place depends on an unspoken agreement about which people are hosts and owners and which are visitors or transients. If, for example, a neighborhood, traditionally dominated by Italian-Americans and kept under surveillance by Italian-American merchants is invaded by Hispanic people, a contest may ensue for economic control, ownership, and other power. At this point it is quite unclear who gives way to whom on the streets, in the shops, and at all thresholds from location to neighborhood zones.

Furthermore, one kind of people may live in a place built for the life styles of another. In fact, convention and control may differ at all levels of the hierarchy. Suppose, for example, that a Hispanic family lives in an apartment complex of Jewish ownership in an Italian-American neighborhood in a predominantly Irish and Italian-Catholic region in a British-American city. At each level there will be a question of incongruent customs and mixed and conflicting aegis.

The Incongruence of Form and Idea

When people experience territorial distortion, they may in some measure accommodate to it. They also use the regulatory behavior described in Chapter 20 and sometimes they even try to straighten out problems in the larger contexts. *But characteristically, western peoples tend to attribute uncustomary behavior to the instincts and personalities of those who reflect the disturbance.* Thus they lose sight of the larger contexts of disturbance and "biologize"—reduce a broad hierarchical problem to simplistic biological-psychological explanations—"or "psychologize" a broad hierarchical problem.

A psychology of territoriality has evolved, for instance. In this view the emphasis is placed almost entirely on how people *feel about* space and crowding. If focus can be centered on feelings about space rather than on territoriality itself, it becomes possible to use persuasion, propaganda, psychotherapy, and other approaches to get people to feel they have enough space and an adequate territorial system, when in fact they do not. Then, when residential areas are sacrificed for commercial buildings, or expressways are used to splinter a neighborhood or wall off a ghetto, the protesters' attention can be diverted to an interest in how they feel. They can be made to feel that they have representation and even that they are to blame for the problem!

Those who biologize territoriality—i.e. explain it *solely* in genetic terms—can put the shoe on the other foot. They can rationalize conquerors and master races, for instance. In either case, the academic who creates another reductionistic explanation or another high sounding rationale is extraordinarily useful to those who take living space from the poor or the elderly in order to build office buildings and other commercial properties.

There is another disturbing tradition that emerges from the ability to confuse meta-conceptions of territoriality and the actual form and organization of space. Some people with bizarre notions of territory have the facility to be able to rationalize their uses of space on a meta-physical or aesthetic basis. In this case their deviant ideas strike us as creative genius rather than deviance. So we commission such people to build spaces that look like projections of God, or whatever. That the spaces are unusable or that they dismember relationships and social groupings is overlooked. One architect told us that his assistants were aesthetic geniuses and that people just had to get used to "beautiful places."

But the distinction between exploitation and creative adaptation is not easy for any of us to make. Those who create and build uncustomary spaces may reflect an atavistic streak or herald a new evolutionary invention.

It is critical, then, that we not stop our inquiry into uncustomary territoriality with a discussion of deviance. We must inquire about its contexts.

The Significance of Territorial Disruption

Evidence has been published that territorial disruption among non-human animals results in social disorganization and violence and in deviant behavior and endocrine disorders.* Similar relationships have been postulated in the case of man. Overcrowding has been blamed for violence and territorial disputes have been blamed for crime and for wars. Actually, we do not yet understand the complex relations between territorial organization and social problems and health.

Porterfield ** has amassed statistical evidence that violence (as measured by crime, murder, and automobile accidents), increases in all states of the U. S. and in all countries of the world *in direct proportion to the degree of cultural heterogeneity.* It is well known that peoples sharing the same territory blame one another for violence therein. In the United States minority groups are blamed for the high violence rates. Yet in these areas of high heterogeneity, there is also a tendency toward crowding, poverty, and mixed and confused jurisdiction and aegis. Newman's figures show that violence is related to ambiguity in territorial boundaries and a lack of surveillance by the people themselves. And in culturally heterogeneous areas the high murder rates are among people of the same background. The residents in these areas still *kill their own kind rather than one another.*

In short, we will have to examine complex systems relations if we are to understand and combat violence, crime, deviance, and ill-health.

---

* Calhoun (1966).
** Porterfield (1965).

references

BIRDWHISTLE, R. L., Some relation between American kinesics and spoken American English. In Smith, A. G. (ed.), *Communication and Culture*. New York: Holt, Rinehart & Winston, 1966.

———, *Kinesics and Context*. Philadelphia: University of Pennsylvania Press, 1970.

CALHOUN, J. R., Population density and social pathology. *J. Social Issues*. 22(4):46–59, 1966.

CHARNY, E. J., Postural configurations in psychotherapy. *Psychosom. Med*. 28:305–315 (July), 1966.

CONDON, W. S. and OGSTON, W. D., Sound film analyses of normal and pathological behavior patterns, *J. Nerv. & Ment. Dis*. 143:338–347 (October), 1966.

EIBL-EIBESFELDT, I., *Ethology: The Biology of Behavior*. New York: Holt, Rinehart & Winston, 1970.

FLOYD, K., *Of time and the mind*. The Academy (American Academy of Psychoanalysis) 18(4):11 (November), 1974.

GIOSCIA, V., *Time Forms. Vol. I. Varieties of Temporal Experience*. New York: Gordon and Breach, 1974.

GOFFMAN, E., *Behavior in Public Places*. Glencoe, Illinois: The Free Press, 1963.

HALL, E. T., A system for the rotation of proxemic behavior. *Amer. Anthropol*. 65:1003–1026, 1963.

———, *The Hidden Dimension*. Garden City, New York: Doubleday, 1966.

HARRIS, M., *The Nature of Cultural Things*. New York: Random House, 1964.

KENDON, A., *Formation Systems*. To be published, 1976.

———, Movement coordination in social interaction. *Acta Psychologica.* 32:100–125, 1970.

———, Personal communication, 1972, 1973.

———, The role of visible behavior in the organization of social interaction. In VonCranach, M. and Vine, I. (eds.), *Movement and Social Communication in Man and Chimpanzee*. London and New York: Academic Press, 1973.

——— and FERBER, A., A description of some behavior and greetings. In Michael, R. P. and Cook, J. H. (eds.), *Comparative Ecology and Behavior of Primates*. London, Academic Press, 1974.

KOUWENHOVEN, J. A., *The Columbia Historical Portrait of New York*. New York: Harper and Row, 1953.

LORENZ, K., *On Aggression*. Trans. by M. Wilson. New York: Harcourt, Brace, Jovanovich, 1966.

McBRIDE, G., *A General Theory of Social Organization and Behavior*. St. Lucia, Australia: University of Queensland Press, 1964.

McMILLAN, R., "Analysis of Multiple Events in a Ghetto Household." Doctoral Thesis. New York: Teachers College, Columbia University, 1974.

NEWMAN, O., *Defensible Space*. New York: Macmillan, 1972.

PORTERFIELD, A. L., *Cultures of Violence*. Fort Worth, Texas: Potishman Foundation, 1965.

SCHEFLEN, A. E., *Body Language and The Social Order*. Englewood Cliffs, New Jersey: Prentice-Hall, 1972.

———, The significance of posture in communication systems. *Psychiat.* 27:316–331 (November), 1964.

———, *The Stream and Structure of Communicational Behavior*. Revised Edition. Bloomington, Indiana: University of Indiana Press, 1973.

——— and ASHCRAFT, N., *Space Distortions—Problems in Human Territoriality*. Doubleday, 1976.

SOMMER, R., *Personal Space*. Englewood Cliffs, New Jersey: Prentice-Hall, 1969.

WYNNE-EDWARDS, J. E., *Animal Dispersion in Relation to Social Behavior*. New York: Hafner, 1962.

glossary

Activity Stage: A portion of a traditional human affair which is carried out while the participants remain in a particular place *and hold a particular formation.* For example, the participants at a dinner party take seats in the dining area and remain there while they eat. Then they adjourn to the living room for another stage of conversation. A stage is made up of phases, which in turn are made up of steps (see phases and steps).

Area: A portion of space roughly equivalent to the size of one domestic room. In the British–American tradition this space is about 15 x 18 or 22 square English feet. It may be as small as the size of a traditional nucleus, i.e., about 9 x 12 feet.

Assembly Space: An increment of space used by and claimed by any group of people who assemble for a particular activity.

Base: A complex of areas held by a particular social group and used as a base for their operations. The house and the small industrial shops are examples.

Built Territory: Any claimed and defended space that is outfitted with fences, walls and other built features.

Channel: The space between the bodies of two or more people who are facing each other and engaged in interaction.

Closed Mutual Orientation: A relationship between two or more people who are highly involved with each other. They ignore others and use their bodies to exclude others from the space of their interaction.

Complex: A set of multiple residential bases, together with common entrances, lobbies and storage areas, e.g., the apartment house.

Connection: Any relation between activities of the body parts of two or more people, e.g., contact by touch, exchange of words or mutual gazes. See "link" and "tie" as particular forms of connection.

Context: The context of any particular event is the totality of larger events within which that event occurs. A context is thus a system of events. It is not a physical setting or an environment.

Co-point: A relation in which two or more people orient a body part in common and thus address the same focus of observation or action. A co-point sequence is a succession of actions in common. For example, two people may look at a third, wave to him, and then call to him in unison.

Co-presence or Co-present Relationship: A relationship in which two or more people take locations in the same area but do not attend to each other. For example, those who are passengers in a public conveyance are simply co-present.

Cubit Space: A space about 18 x 18 x 18 inches—adequate for the use of one body region. The old English cubit it about 18 inches. In other cultures and in contemporary America the cubit is likely to be 24 inches or more in each dimension.

Disassociation: A state of relationship in which those present actively avoid engagement, coaction and interaction.

Dyad: A pair of people who are obviously with each other; acting in common or highly involved with each other and sharing the same location.

"E"-formation: An array of people who are oriented in the same direction and clustered in such a way that they form a line, a file, an arc or a square.

Element: An "e" formation which is one element or part of some larger formation. Thus if two rows of people face each other each row is an element in the total cluster. In the parade each band or marching group is an element in the parade. One person can be an element if he or she occupies one side of the formation and is oriented alone in a particular direction.

"F"-Formation: A relationship of participants in which two or more people or elements *face each other.* Thus the "f" or face formation consists of two or more "e" formations or elements in mutual involvement.

Face Formation: See "F" formation above.

Frame: A boundary in space and time. Spacially the frame is formed by the assembly of people and/or chairs and the like within which a human activity will occur. Temporally the frame is initiated when the participants begin a phase or stage of the activity and the frame is terminated when they complete the activity and turn to something else.

"G"-Formation: A formation of people or furnishings which has multiple centers of activity. Thus the "G" formation or gathering is made up of multiple elements and/or face formations. A common example

is the cocktail party at which several conversations are occurring simultaneously in different portions of the area.

Gathering: See "G" formation.

Gating: The system of barriers and constraints by which entrance and exit to and from a territory is selectively controlled. Gating permits some people to enter a territory on some occasions for some purposes.

"H"-Formation: A formation of people, furniture, or built spaces which has concentric zones and therefore takes the shape of a hub or a slice of a hub. Each concentric zone is gated for the use of particular people for particular roles. Rings of supporters and spectators around a central performer is an example which occurs in open sites. The amphitheater or stadium is a built example.

High Commitment: A relationship in which the participants are engrossed with a common task or each other. In a configuration of high commitment the participants have leaned or moved close to the focus and committed multiple body parts to this focus. Thus they listen, see, touch, speak to and generally orient multiple body regions to the activity. This configuration is seen in intense rapport, courtship and confrontation.

Hold: In this volume the word "hold" has been used as a noun to designate a mutual engagement of body parts which is maintained or held for an interval of time. Thus the maintenance of hand contact or mutual gazes is a hold.

Hub: See "H" Formation above.

"k" Space: A constant representing the minimum space occupied by an adult human body. This space is about four cubic cubits or about 1.5 X 1.5 X 6 English feet.

Level of Point Units: A level of observation at which one can see or hear the behavior of a single body part, i.e., the brow, eyes, mouth, hand, foot, etc. The point unit is one sequence of behavior performed by a body part and the space used in this performance.

Level of Positional Unit: A level at which one can observe the behavior of a body region (or two or more body regions if these are used collectively in the same orientation and behavioral sequence).

Level of Positions: See Level of Positional Units.

Link: A unit of mutual behavior which links the eyes, mouths, hands or other body parts of two or more people together during interaction, e.g., an exchange of glances or mutual displays of the palm. The link, which is formed by an interaction, is distinguished from the tie (see below). Both are forms of connection.

Location: The space occupied by one person or sometimes by a dyad at any moment of time. This space is often about one square yard in floor or ground area but it varies with activity, relationship, density, culture and other contextual states.

Low Commitment: A state of a relationship in which the parties are not highly involved or affiliated with each other. The configuration of low commitment is characterized by using large interpersonal distances, orienting in different directions, forming few connections, folding and crossing the arms and legs and so forth.

Meta-territorial Activity: Activity about territories such as planning, negotiating. mapping and describing territories and problems of territoriality.

Module: An increment of bounded space which consists of a row of locations, e.g., a row of seats, rooms, connected houses on a street or city blocks along a main highway.

Mutual Orientation: A relationship of orientations in which the body parts, regions or whole bodies of two or more people are turned *to each other.*

Non-witness: See Co-presence.

Nuclear Formation: An assemblage or formation which occupies the center of a territory. A nuclear formation may occupy the geographic center of a room, house, building complex, block, neighborhood or town, or it may occupy the center of activity as in the case of performers on a stage.

Nuclear Space: The space at the geographic center or center of activity in a territory.

Nucleus: See Nuclear Space and Nuclear Formation.

Orientational Field: The total space covered for a time by the orientations of a person or a group of people. In the case of an element the orientational field lies in front of the person or row of people. In the case of a face formation the orientational field lies primarily between the participants.

Orientational Hold: The action of orienting and holding the orientation of the body or of a bodily part until a certain action is completed. An orientational hold may be shared by a number of people.

Orientational Segment: The sector of space commanded by the orientation of a single person.

"O" Rights: Rights to enter the open space at the center of the nucleus of a territory. In territories the size of an area this right would allow a person to stand between two or more people in conversation or to sit upon a central table. In larger territories "o" rights allow entry to a court, stage, arena, central hall, lobby, town square, central park, or commons.

"O" Space: The most central zone of the nucleus of a territory. The "o" zone lies within the "p" zone or zone of main participation. In a conversational cluster, for instance, the "o" zone is the central open space between sofas and chairs. In the dining cluster the "o" zone is occupied by the table. In larger territories the "o" zone is a central hall, lobby, arena, stage, court, square or park.

"O" Zone: See "O" Space.

Parallel or Congruent Postures: A relation among the postures or stances of several people in which all are holding their bodies and extremities in the same way.

Phase: An interval of time in which certain activities are carried out in sequence. Thus the phase is a segment of activity within a stage. The phase is in turn made up of steps. During a phase the same general orientations and positions are held by the participants.

Place Distortion: A change in the customary setting, shape, or furnishing of territory which disrupts or alters the activities which occur there.

Point: A micro behavior carried out by some body part, oriented, directed or pointed to a certain person, group or focus.

Point Behavior: See Point.

Point Unit: A sequence of point behavior forming a recognizable unit of behavior. This point unit, too, is oriented and thus defines a small, temporary territory.

Polarity: The directionality of a group orientation or place arrangement. In a central polarity the people, furniture units, rooms or buildings are oriented to face a central "o" space. In a peripheral or centrifugal polarity these units face away from the center as they do in the kitchen or in a shop. Subunits may also face the front or the back of a built territory as they do in an auditorium.

Positional Unit or Position: The orientation of a body region is held while a sequence of point behaviors are carried out. The total positional unit is a complex of these behaviors, The orientation and the space into which the behavior is projected.

"P" Rights: The rights to enter and use the second zone of the nucleus. The "p" zone is that zone which is used by the central participants in a face to face or hub type of formations such as conversation or theatrical performance. In built territories the "p" zone is a zone of main chairs, rooms, buildings, blocks or neighborhoods. "P" rights are thus roughly equivalent to those of a main participant or performer.

"P" Space or "P" Zone: The second space of the nucleus immediately surrounding the central, open zone.

"Q" Space or "Q" Zone: The space just beyond or around the "p" zone of a nucleus. The "q" zone, if present, is thus the third or most peripheral of the nuclear zones. In the dining room the "q" space lies behind the chairs allowing room to enter and leave them.

Region: The peripheral space or zone of a territory; the space or zone lying peripheral to the nucleus. The region may be subdivided into an inner zone, "r" (which gives location to coaches. substitutes, referees, advisors and other supportive people) an outer zone, "s" for spectators, and sometimes a third even more peripheral zone, "t" for passage, gatekeepers and vehicles.

Relation: The term has been used in this volume to refer in particular to inter-relations between the behavior of body parts and body regions. It is thus differentiated from the term "relationship" which occurs among the whole bodies of the participants.

"R" Rights: Rights to enter and use the region of a territory.

"R" Space or "R" Zone: See region (the lower case "r" has been used to refer to the innermost subzone when the region is subdivided into region, spectator zone and transit zone).

Sector: A bounded portion of a linear or non-concentric territory.

Segment: A portion of a spacial whole or of a subsequence of activity.

Set-up: A grouping or cluster of furniture.

Site: The unbuilt space in which a human event occurs.

Site-event: A spacio-temporal construct to define both the sequence of activity at a site and the site itself.

Site Form: The location, shape and layout of a site.

Site-occasion: The time at which a particular site is occupied and used.

Space-time Unit: The totality of occurrences which happen at a particular site or place during a particular interval of time.

Spot: A micro-territory, inches in diameter. Some spots are located on the body surface, e.g., the eyes, brow, mouth and palms. Some are imaginary foci at which people direct gaze or voice. Some spots appear on furniture and are used for storing objects.

"S" Rights: Rights to use the outer portion of the region of a territory. "S" rights are usually those of spectators or customers.

Stage: See Activity Stage.

Stance: The postural form of a body region or of the body as a whole including the body orientation, the set or expression and the positioning of the extremities.

Step: A short sequence of behavior occurring in some phase of a human activity. The duration of a step is marked by holding the orientation and stance of some body regions until that step of activity has been completed.

Surround: A general term for the spaces which immediately surround the region of a territory or the territory as a whole.

Territorial Behavior: Any behavior which claims, bounds, respects, defends or otherwise defines a territory.

Territorial Field: A temporo-spacial construct which describes the form and dimensions of a territory through time. (See Chapter 12.)

Territorial Manipulation: Any behavior which attempts to alter the form, boundaries, ownership or rights to a territory.

Territory: A bounded space claimed, occupied or used by a person or a group for an interval of time.

Tie: A form of connection between body parts or body regions by which people demonstrate that they are with each other. The tie is a co-actional behavior while the link is an interactive one.

"T"-Right: The right to pass through the periphery of a territory. In the case of larger territories a path for public transit may cut through the center of the territory. In this case T-Rights allow passage through the territory itself.

"T"-Space or "T"-Zone: That portion of a territory or that zone in a concentric territory through which strangers are allowed to pass.

"u" Relation: A relation in which two or more people orient body regions in common and coact.

"U" Relationship: A relationship in which two or more people orient their whole bodies in common and coact in concert toward the object of their orientation.

"U" Right: A right to take location near another person, share his or her orientation and coact with him. This right is ordinarily awarded to fellow travellers and fellow spectators.

"U" Space: The space commanded by unison or common orientations. The behaviors of coaction are projected into this space.

Unit of Relation: The totality of orientational and other behavoir which is shared whenever two or more people bring body regions into a shared action. The unit begins when the first participant adopts the position and ends when the last participant abandons it.

Unit of Relationship: A shared positioning of the entire bodies of two or more people.

"v" relation: A mutual relation between two or more people in which only one or two body regions are brought face to face.

"V" Relationship: A mutual relationship of whole bodies in which the participants orient to each other and interact.

"V" Right: The right to enter into face to face relations with another person or group. This right is ordinarily granted to acquaintances, friends, relatives and business associates, but not to strangers.

"V" Space: The space between those who are oriented to each other.

"v" Space: The space between body regions which face each other.

With or "W" Relationship: A configuration ordinarily shown by those who are affiliated or together. The configuration is evidenced by clustering together, coacting and/or interacting, using parallel postures and synchronous movements and often by mutual touch.

"w" relation: A "with" relation shared only by certain of the body regions of the participants.

With or "W" Right: The right to enter a "with" relation or "with" relationship. This right is ordinarily afforded only to people who are affiliated. Strangers are to maintain a distance, employ a different orientation and stance, and keep their gazes and voices out of a "with" space.

With or "W" Space: The space between those who are with each other. Often this space is defined by the placement of arms and legs. (See Chapter 5).

"X" Relationship: A relationship which demonstrates non-affiliation. It is characterized by relative interpersonal distance and the use of different orientations, activities and stances.

"x" Relation: A constellation of non-affiliation involving only certain bodily parts.

"Y" Relationship: The relationship which obtains between those who occupy different zones of a territory and thus have different statuses at that time. A Y relationship occurs between performers and spectators and between sales people and customers.

"Y" Rights: The right to enter the peripheral zone or sector of a territory *and* relate to those who hold a more central or nuclear position.

Zone: One of the spaces in a concentrically organized territory.

"Z" Relationship: The relationship which obtains between those who occupy a territory and those who are ordinarily excluded.

In Sum

The letters: A,B,C, and D code levels of territorial organizations;
The letters: E,F, G,H and I code customary types of human formations or clusters;
The letters: K, L, M and N code increments of territory;
The letters: O,P,Q,R,S and T code zones or sectors of a territory;
The letters: U,V,W,X,Y and Z code type of relationship among the participants of a group.